Beneath Her Cracked Armor She Blooms
The Power, Pain & Poetry of A Black Woman

NaKiyah LaJoi

Copyright © 2024 NaKiyah LaJoi

All rights reserved.

ISBN: 9798340186133

DEDICATION

This book is dedicated to my mother, my grandmother Ozella, my Aunt Freda, my best friend Nicole, my good friend Tink, my sister Yana, and my brother Bishop—may you all rest in peace. Your love, wisdom, and strength continue to guide me, and this book is a tribute to the legacies you've left behind.

I also dedicate this book to every young girl who dares to dream, to every girl who has ever been told she wasn't enough. You are more than enough, and I hope these pages remind you of the power you carry within.

And to the grown-ass Black women on their journey—those who have faced obstacles, overcome battles, and continue to rise—this book is for you. It's a celebration of your strength, your resilience, and your evolution. Let this be a reminder that we are all blooming, no matter where we are in life.

ACKNOWLEDGMENTS	ix
Introduction	1
DARE TO RISE	3
B-L-A-C-K W-O-M-E-N	6
GOD HAS GOT TO BE A BLACK WOMAN	7
To the Womb of the Black Mother	10
The Birth	12
From Labor to the Morgue	14
HER BIRTHRIGHT	17
To the Life We Build	19
Beads and Bows	23
Pity Patters	26
Tough Love	30
The Way, They See Us	34
FITTING IN	37
"First Pair of Heels"	40
Dear Black Daughter of the World,	42
GRANNY'S MAC & CHEESE AND FRIED CHICKEN	45
Apples Tree Roots	48
Her Life, My Lesson	51
His Hats, Boots, and Absence	54
What They Took	56
Chasing Love in the Dark	62
To The Boy Whose Mama Called My House	68
Roots That Hold	70
Her First-Born Son	73
"Raising Him in a World Not Built for Him"	76

Mirror- Mirror	78
Chasing Love in the Dark"	81
ROADMAPS in my REARVIEW	84
Made for the Storm	88
NEW SKIN	90
The Color of My Voice"	92
Say it Again	96
Ode to Old School	98
Everybody's favorite Auntie	101
THE ENGINE THAT KEEPS RUNNING"	104
Stress be Killing US, sis	107
Hands that Heal	111
are learning to carry me	113
RELAX, REST, AND RESET	114
Sacred Ground	116
Get up queen	117
LEMONADE & HEALING	119
UNCHAIN ME	120
Unapologizing	123
Steps To Not Giving A F*ck	125
God Gave You Dominion Over the Earth	128
Crooklyn	131
Standing Alone	133
The Art of Petty	135
I'm Fine"	138
Monsters	141

Check on Your Strong Friend	144
BEATING THE FACE TO COVER THE BEATING	146
Heaviness Carries the Heart	150
My Sister Got Me	152
Roses Can Grow in Strange Places	154
She Tends to Herself	156
How to Love When You're Broken	159
Beneath Her Cracked Armor, She Blooms	163
Black Heart Laughter	166
Look Good, Feel Good	169
Love Letter to My Stretch Marks	172
These Jeans Got Stories	174
Afros and Almond Butter	176
The Little Black Dress	179
Sweeter and Seasoned	181
Golden, Not Just Pretty	183
Built Like That	185
Brown Sugar Honey Pot	189
Red Lipstick	191
Now, i understand	194
That Ain't That	197
"All That Energy"	200
Date 'em all sis	202
"Why We Don't Text Back"	205
"Swipe Left on Red Flags"	208
I ain't married, but if i was	212

"Men Are Not Projects"	216
"Love Looks Different Now"	218
"I Know Why I Still Sing"	220
Where My girls at	223
willie Lynch and Us	226
armor in excellence	230
For Kamala and the Sisters in Power	237
We Want What's Owed	240
Currency and Change	244
A Black Woman's Voice & Choice	247
missing without a sound	250
a Black Woman that Lives on the Sun	254
A Black Woman's Prayers	257
ABOUT THE AUTHOR	260

ACKNOWLEDGMENTS

First, I give all glory and thanks to God, the Creator and Ruler of the heavens and earth, for the countless blessings I receive daily. I thank God for His son, Christ Jesus, who died on the cross for little ole me. I'm forever grateful for His mercy and grace that covers, carries, and lifts me up when I fall. I don't know where I would be without His love and promises. I am so thankful for the gift of writing—a gift that has been my refuge and helped me through the darkest moments of my life. As Isaiah 30:8 says: "And now, go, write it before them on a tablet and inscribe it in a book, that it may be for the time to come as a witness forever." This book is my witness.

To My Beautiful Children
You are the foundation of everything I am. Each of you carries a piece of my heart into this world. I haven't always been the best version of myself, so I apologize. But you are my greatest achievement, source of joy, and why I fight to improve every day. I love you more than words could ever express, and I believe in you with everything I have.

Marcus, my firstborn, my heart.
Your strength and wisdom have always been beyond your years. You've taught me more about humility, perseverance, and true belief in oneself than I could ever teach you. You joke that you're "85% right," and honestly? You're not far off. Your sharp mind, strong instincts, and relentless drive amaze me. You have a gift for seeing opportunities where others see

obstacles. I know you were born for greatness, but in all your success, never forget the humility that keeps you grounded. You lift others up without even knowing it, and that, my son, is the real mark of a great man. I love you and am so proud of who you are and the man you're becoming.

Trinity, my one and only daughter, my mirror, my heart.
Every day I watch you, I am in awe. You've faced challenges that would break most, but you rise every time—with grace, power, and determination. I'm sorry for the times I couldn't be all you needed but know this—you have always been everything to me. You are a force of nature, defying odds with every step you take. Now, as a mother yourself, I am beyond proud of how you love and protect your own. Never doubt your strength or your worth. You are royalty, my legacy, and I love you fiercely.

Bishop, my baby boy.
Mommy loves you more than words can describe. You came into our lives with a purpose; every day, you live out that purpose in ways that make me so proud. Never let the world define you. Be who you are unapologetically. Your voice, your heart, your mind—they matter. Stay faithful to God, and know that He will always stay faithful to you, just as He promised. Bishop, your wisdom and maturity at 11 years old are beyond anything I've ever seen. You speak your mind with a clarity and honesty that's rare, and I admire you for it. You have so much to offer this world, and I can't wait to see what you'll accomplish as you grow. Keep being brave, keep seeking answers, and never stop being the incredible young man you are. You are a force, and I believe in you with everything I've got.

Aunt Gwen, thank you for always being there for me and our entire family. We wouldn't have made it this far without the sacrifices you've made for all of us. Thank you for always encouraging me to follow my dreams and reminding me never to let go of writing. Your wisdom has been a guiding light.

Aunt Jocie, you've always been a steady presence in my life. No matter what, you're always there, supporting me and lifting me up. Thank you for being my golden honey, your endless support, and always being present when I needed you most.

To the "Cousin Crew,"
My sisters in spirit and in love. I love each of you fiercely. Together, we've broken the generational cycles and curses that tried to plague our family, and I'm so proud of us for that. You ladies wear the title of "mother" with such ease and grace, and I admire each one of you.

Lennette, hey girl hey!
I love your Leo ass so much, hunty. You've taught me so many lessons in this life. You've been by my side through everything—lifting me up with that fiery spirit of yours, always ready to push, uplift, and challenge me to be my best self. I admire how you walk through this world, head held high, never letting anyone dim your shine. You've reminded me, time and time again, to embrace my own strength and never settle for anything less than I deserve. I will cherish you always.

Carlette,
You are hands down the funniest and sweetest woman I know. Watching you turn your passions into a full-blown lifestyle and brand has been nothing short of inspiring. How you've live your life with grace, humor, and determination is beautiful to

witness. I can't wait for the day I walk into your restaurant, sit down, and order that first meal, knowing how much heart and soul went into every detail. @eatyourheartout729 will blow up, and I will be front row, cheering you on every step of the way. I'm so proud of you.

Lacy,
I think back to us as kids, sitting in your room, talking about dreams that felt so big back then. Look at us now! I'm so proud to call you my cousin. You've taken those dreams and turned them into something real, something powerful. You inspire my entrepreneurial spirit daily with how you move and build. Dream reflects everything you are—beautiful, driven, and true to your purpose. I couldn't be prouder to watch you shine and do your thing.

Tia,
You're the one I can sit on the phone with for hours, talking about everything and nothing simultaneously. The hustler of all hustlers—girl, you've got that grind in your DNA. Just let me write the book for you already! I love you, and no matter how far apart we are or how much time passes, that bond will never change. I can't wait to see what the future holds for you—catch those dreams, sis, because they're yours for the taking. I know I'm gonna see your name in lights one day, and I'll be right there, smiling from ear to ear.

Jalesa,
You've been riding with me for years, always supporting my writing and my journey. We've been through a lot together, and I'll never forget the times you held my secrets close and gave me the space to grow. Thank you for always being there and for never letting me down. I love you, and I'm so excited for this next chapter in your life with Jalina. Let's make sure we don't

let too much time slip between us. You're family forever.

Bre,
My baby, Look at you a mother and a teacher. You have been through hell and back and don't look like it. If you ain't your mama's child. Your sons are blessed to have you queen. Keep your foot on the gas. Love you.

Taylor,
My daughter from another mother, you have no idea how proud I am of you. You are a sweet, kind soul with a talent that shines through in everything you do. The world is truly yours for the taking; whatever you set your heart and mind to, you can achieve it. Your gift is beyond anything I've seen. I can't wait to hear your album, and one day soon, I'll be sitting in the front row on Broadway, watching you live out your dreams, baby girl. Keep pushing because the sky isn't even your limit.

Leah,
Our fashionista queen! Never forget who you are and where you come from. Your smile is like sunshine—bright, radiant, and capable of lighting up any room you walk into. Keep living your life boldly, on your terms, and never let anyone dim that light. I'm so proud of the woman you're becoming, and no matter where life takes us, let's stay connected, cousin! You're a force, and I'll always be cheering you on.

Tamera and Tambra,
I love both of you so deeply. They say there's always a pot of gold at the end of the rainbow, and that's exactly what the two of you are—our gold. Let's keep building together, creating a legacy for generations. Family is everything, and I'm grateful to have you by my side as we travel this journey together.

Jennifer,
Cousinnnn, thank you for always checking in on me and being

that quiet but constant presence in my life. Your love and care mean the world to me, and I want you to know I love you so much. You've been a rock, and I'm so thankful for you.

Ma Ruth,
I honestly don't know where I'd be today if it hadn't been for you. You've been an angel in my life—here on earth, guiding me when I needed it most. I thank God every day for you. You're truly a blessing, and I'll never be able to describe how much you mean to me.

Mecaela "Cae" Dunson,
You will forever be my sister in every sense of the word. I love you so much. I pray that true love, pure love, finds you, because you deserve nothing less. Thank you for always having my back and for loving me in ways nobody else could.

Mommy Rosa,
Mamita, I love you dearly. Thank you for your wisdom, your support, and for being the mother I didn't even know I needed. You've loved me without condition, always keeping your door open and your heart even wider. I'm so blessed to have you in my life, and I'm forever grateful for your love.

Solomia,
My sister from another mister! I thank God for you. Some of my best memories, my most cherished stories, have you in them. You've taught me so much—lessons I still carry with me to this day. You've given me love, laughter, and guidance, and for that, I'll always be grateful. I love you!

Brittnee,
My best friend, my sister for life. You are truly a jewel, rare and priceless. I still remember the day you walked into my life, and

from that moment on, we've been locked in, no questions asked. I've never had to doubt our sisterhood, and that's something special. On the Code, we're in this together forever.

Aija,
My sister, we've walked through life's chaos together. Our friendship is a testament to forgiveness, redemption, and raw, unfiltered truth. I cherish you and everything we've been through—it's made us who we are.

Darvincia,
My soul sister. I've never had a friend like you before. You've been that unexpected shoulder to lean on, my biggest cheerleader in this entrepreneurial journey, and a blessing in my life. Truly, God sent you to me, and for that, I'll always be grateful. You've shown me what true sisterhood looks like, and I love that you! lol

To Shanika and the Hardy Girls, My Sister Girls
Shanika, we've been through it all since way back, from childhood friends to family. You've been by my side through many moons, and I couldn't be more grateful for the love and familyhood we've built.

To the Hardy girls—my sisters, too—you've become a part of my heart and soul. You all bring so much joy, laughter, and love into my life. It's rare to find people who feel like home, but that's what y'all are to me. We've built a sisterhood that will last forever, and I'm beyond blessed to have you all in my life.

To My Sisters, Family, and Every Woman Who's Made an Impact
To my other sisters, cousins, friends, extended family, and the women who have touched my life in ways that words could

never fully capture—NeNe, Imani, Jeloni, Wendy, Robyn, LaKeisha, Jessica (BB), Carla, Ms. Q, Tracey Burton, Erica, Oneisha, Ma Meka, Mother Taji Anderson, India, Destiny, Mama Pat, Samantha Simpore, Dana(sista-sista)—you each hold a special place in my heart. If I've mentioned you by name, know that our bond is something I cherish deeply. At some point in my life, you've lifted me up, inspired me, or simply been there when I needed it most. You've made a difference, and I am forever grateful for you.

A special shout-out to my uncles, the men who've helped shape me, supported me, and always reminded me what it means to have strong family bonds. Whether it was a word of encouragement, a shoulder to lean on, or just knowing you were there, your presence in my life has been invaluable. Thank you for being there, for lifting me up, and for always having my back.

And to my readers—you, too, are family now. Through these pages, we've shared a journey, and I hope you feel the love, strength, and sisterhood that comes with it. We are stronger than we know, braver than we believe, and more powerful than we've ever been told. Never forget the beauty in your strength, the grace in your resilience, and the love that you carry inside you. I'm proud of each of you, and I hope this book reminds you that we are all connected, we are all blooming, and we are all worthy of love and greatness.

With all my love and respect—thank you for being part of my journey. We're family now, and I'm forever grateful for each of you

INTRODUCTION

For so long, I didn't feel like I had a voice. I know I'm not alone in that—so many of us, Black women, have been silenced in one way or another. We're told to hold our tongues, to push through pain, to bear the weight of the world without complaint. But silence doesn't mean we don't have stories to tell. I wrote *Beneath Her Cracked Armor She Blooms* because I refuse to let my voice—and the voices of other Black women—remain unheard any longer.

This book is a celebration of us—our strength, our resilience, our journeys. It's for the Black women who have walked through fire and found a way to rise. It's for the women who have loved fiercely, survived trauma, and are on a path to healing. These poems come from my own personal experiences and the stories of the women who have shaped my life. Every woman I've known—whether she's my sister, my friend, or someone I crossed paths with for just a moment—has added something to this collection. I've written these poems with all of us in mind.

On these pages, you'll find pieces of yourself. Whether you're young or old, a mother, a sister, a daughter, or just a woman navigating this world, there's something here for you. This book is a journey of self-discovery, healing, and reclamation. We'll touch on motherhood, mental health, the scars left by slavery, toxic relationships, and the bonds of sisterhood that hold us together when the world tries to tear us apart.

It's time we celebrate Black women for the queens we are. We've been through battles we didn't ask for, but we've come out the other side and earned the right to tell our stories in our own voices. This book is about peeling off the layers of strength we've worn as armor, embracing our vulnerability, and remembering that beneath it all, we are blooming. We are powerful, we are beautiful, and we are worthy.

So, as you read these poems, I invite you to join me on this journey. Let's walk together through the pain, the joy, the lessons, and the love. Let's celebrate the Black woman in all her complexity—her strength, softness, resilience, and grace. Because beneath our cracked armor, we all have the power to bloom.

.

DARE TO RISE

This is for us,
the ones who stand
    on the shoulders of giants,
for the daughters of the soil,
descendants of queens and warriors,
    who wake up every day tired
  with the weight of the world on their backs,
but still

find the strength to rise,
with fire in their eyes.

For the women who carry universes in their wombs,
    who bend but don't break,
who take what life gives them—
    sometimes too little, sometimes too late—
and turn it ALL into gold,
    despite all the weight.

This is for every Black woman
    who's been told she was too much,
or somehow not enough,
who was made to feel like she had to be soft,
    but was **forged in fire, tough**.

Who was told to keep quiet,
> but learned to **roar**,
> with a heart that always knew
it was destined for more.

We are not new to this.
We have been loving,
> building,
> healing,
> carving out spaces
where we can be free,
> even when the world tried to cage us completely.

We rise.
Not just for ourselves,
> but for every sister
> whoever felt unseen,
for every mother
> who birthed dreams
> into a world
that wasn't as kind as it seems.

We are the embodiment of grace under pressure,
> the fire that refuses to be extinguished.
We are the ones who smile through pain,
> who laugh in the face of adversity,
knowing that strength is not just in survival—
> but in **thriving**.

This journey is ours.
Each poem is a reflection
> of our stories, our truths,
> our beauty, our power.

Let this be a reminder to every Black woman reading this—
    that you are more than enough,
that your worth cannot be measured
    by the world's standards,
because **you are a force**.

You are a testament
    to everything
that has ever dared to grow
    in the face of destruction.

So let us walk this path
    together,
    boldly,
    unapologetically,
knowing that our steps are guided
    by the legacy of those who came before,
and that the future is ours to restore.

B-L-A-C-K W-O-M-E-N

Born from struggle, but never weak,

Lifting worlds with hands that have seen it all.

All the weight we carry, still walking tall.

Chaos all around, but we create peace.

Knowing we are queens, even when they forget.

We bend, but we don't break—

Open hearts, even when we ache.

Magic runs through our veins,

Every challenge met, every victory earned.

Never defeated, always rising, always us.

GOD HAS GOT TO BE A BLACK WOMAN

God has got to be a Black woman.
Not because we need her to be,
but because no one else could carry the weight of the universe
with the ease of a body that knows struggle
and grace in the same breath.

She is the first breath.
     The one who whispered the world into existence,
     her voice deep like oceans,
steady like the rhythm of drums in the distance,
     calling creation to rise.

She moves mountains without effort,
     with hands that know how to heal and command,
     how to build and unmake.

God has got to be a Black woman—
     because who else can hold the universe together,
every star is placed perfectly,
every orbit running its course,
     while still finding time to tend to us,
to breathe life into the tired, the lost, the broken?

She is the architect,
the one who carved rivers into the earth
     and laid the foundations for nations.

Beneath Her Cracked Armor She Blooms

She is history,
carried in the DNA of every Black woman who ever dared to survive.

She is the embodiment of resilience,
the one who holds us together when the world tries to unravel us.
    She is the fire that cannot be extinguished.

Her power is unmatched,
    not in force, but in knowing—
the way she sees all,
    understands all,
yet still holds us close,
    not in spite of our flaws,
    but because of them.

God has got to be a Black woman.
Her patience is endless,
her forgiveness infinite,
    because she knows—
    she knows what it means to be unseen,
    to be misjudged,
    to be misunderstood.

She knows what it is to carry a world
    that doesn't always recognize her worth
but needs her all the same.

She is the mother of mothers,
    the origin of all things,
    the keeper of wisdom older than time itself.

And when she speaks,
    her words bend reality—

not because she forces them to,
but because the universe has always known
her voice is law.

God has got to be a Black woman,
    because only she could hold the paradox
    of love and justice,
    wrath and mercy,
    life and death,
    and still walk with grace through the chaos.

She is not just watching—
    she is here,
    in every breath we take,
    in the way our hearts beat to a rhythm
older than memory,
    in the way we rise,
    even when the world expects us to fall.

She is the beginning and the end.
    The Alpha and Omega.
The creator who sees herself in us—
    and that is why
God has got to be
    a Black woman.

To the Womb of the Black Mother

Before breath met the outside world,
there was you—
a vessel cradling tomorrow,
your walls rich with promise,
holding the secrets of generations.

Within your depths,
the first heartbeat found rhythm,
learning its song from the echoes of ancestors.
You are the first home,
a place of warmth,
where the universe gathers its strength,
whispering to the child you hold:
"Here, you are safe. Here, you are everything."

You are the keeper of beginnings,
where skin learns its hue,
where bone and spirit find their place.
Your silence is full of the stories you know,
of daughters birthed into resilience,
of sons carried with prayers tucked beneath their ribs.

In the dark, you shape more than flesh.
You prepare a soul for what lies ahead,
for a world that may not always hold them with the care
you give so freely.

You stretch, not just to accommodate life,
but to honor the weight of what you carry.
The future grows within you,
nurtured by the strength that runs in your veins,

Beneath Her Cracked Armor She Blooms

like rivers that remember their course
even after the drought.

Before light ever touched their skin,
you gave them the first taste of love,
a love not fragile,
but one that knows how to withstand storms.
You are the beginning,
the soil from which greatness rises.

To the womb of a Black mother,
you are not just a place of creation.
You are the root,
the anchor,
the quiet force that pulls life forward.
In you, dreams take form,
and in you, futures are carved out of the impossible.

They say you bear the weight of the world,
but that's only because you've always known
how to hold it.

The Birth

I didn't come into this world quietly.
I arrived with purpose,
a cry that carried more than breath,
    like thunder breaking across the sky.
I was not just born;
    I landed.
Feet ready to walk the paths
    they tried to hide from me,
hands prepared to touch what the world said was out of reach.

The first thing I felt was the air,
    heavy with promise,
cool against my skin.
The warmth of the womb released me,
    but not without leaving its mark.
I still carry it—
    the strength of where I came from,
    woven deep in the rhythm of my heart.

This world doesn't know me yet,
    but I know it,
like a melody that's always been there,
waiting for me to sing.
    My cry was more than sound;
    it was a beginning.
A moment that told the world:
    I am here.
And nothing will be the same again.

Beneath Her Cracked Armor She Blooms

The Creator didn't speak,
but I felt the words inside me,
like a drumbeat that couldn't be silenced.
    "You are the spark that ignites the dark,
    carry your flame and make it bright.
    This world is yours,
    step into it with all you are."

My skin, rich with history,
    already knew how to stand under the sun,
    how to hold its glow
    without shrinking away.
    I was wrapped in night,
    born from stars that never lost their shine.

I wasn't just a baby,
    I was a message,
sent to claim my place.
    This life, this earth,
would bend around my steps,
    learn my rhythm,
and find me ready.

The birth wasn't the beginning—
    it was the opening of a door.
And now,
    I stand at the threshold,
    not waiting,
    but walking through

From Labor to the Morgue

They tell you childbirth is a miracle,
that bringing life into the world is beautiful—
    but they don't tell us the whole story.
    For Black women, it's a battlefield,
an old war fought on new ground.
    We enter those rooms with hope in our hearts,
but too often, we leave in silence.

The numbers are written in blood:
    three, four times more likely
    to die giving life,
and still, they act like we're making it up,
    like centuries of screams don't echo in the walls.
They don't hear us.
They don't believe us.
It's carved into their training—
    that we're strong enough to bear it,
    to take more,
as if we were built to suffer.
    They treat our pain like a myth,
    something to brush aside,
    like we aren't human,
    like we weren't made of the same breath
    that created the heavens.

God doesn't make mistakes,
but man does,
over and over again.
    They write off our fears,
    and when we say, "It hurts,"

they stare back,
cold as the walls,
and tell us,
    "That's normal."

But there's nothing normal
    about being sent home bleeding,
        only to return with death tapping at the door.
There is nothing normal about hearing,
    "Another C-section,"
not because it's safer for us,
    but because it's easier for them.

They cut us open,
    and what should be sacred,
what should be beautiful,
turns into another number,
    another Black woman lost
    because they didn't listen.

Because they didn't care.

In America,
we're three to four times more likely to die
trying to bring life.
    Our wombs have always been battlefields,
from the first chains to now,
    and still, we fight.

We fight to survive
    in a system never built for us,
walking into those sterile rooms
with one foot already in the grave.
The numbers don't lie—
60% of these deaths could be prevented,

Beneath Her Cracked Armor She Blooms

but they still happen.
Shalon Irving.
Kira Johnson.
    Names whispered,
    names silenced,
and hundreds more we'll never know.

They say,
    "It's just coincidence,"
    "Bad luck."
But when it's us,
when it's always us,
    it's not luck.
It's history, repeating itself,
like an old wound that refuses to heal.
They've been making mistakes with our bodies
    since they chained us to ships,
    since they claimed our wombs for profit.

We're tired of being strong.
    We want to live—
to hold our babies,
    to feel the joy of creation
without death lurking at the door.
We deserve to be heard,
    to be cared for,
    to survive.
    We enter those rooms ready to give life,
and too often,
we leave in silence,
    our bodies cold,
as our babies cry for the mother
they'll never know.

Beneath Her Cracked Armor She Blooms

HER BIRTHRIGHT

She came into this world like a flame,
born from the earth,
wrapped in the arms of a legacy older than time itself.
From the moment she took her first breath,
she was bound to greatness,
carved from the same stone as her foremothers—
women who knew how to hold the sky and still walk with grace.
She carries the wisdom of centuries,
each step she takes a reminder of who she is,
where she's come from.
Her laughter isn't just joy—
it's freedom,
a release from all that tried to hold her back.
Her power doesn't scream;
it's quiet, steady, unyielding,
built on the strength of those who rose before her.
This is her birthright— to walk through the world without apology, to wear her skin with pride, to hold her head high in the face of anything. The world doesn't get to define her— she defines herself.
She's more than what they see.
Every scar she wears, every line on her body,
it's a testament to the battles she's fought,
to the wars won long before she even arrived.
She carries the stories of those who couldn't tell theirs,
of women who built entire worlds from dust.
She moves with purpose,
her roots deep,
her branches wide,
connecting her to everything that ever was,
to everything she's yet to become.
Her spirit is the river,
binding her to the earth and to her sisters.

Beneath Her Cracked Armor She Blooms

When she stands, she lifts them with her,
because rising is never a solo journey.
It's a collective movement.
And love?
It radiates from her like the sun,
healing all that it touches.
She is both the storm and the calm,
a force that can't be caged,
a light that never dims.
Every step forward is a victory,
every laugh, a rebellion.
She is a reminder that power doesn't come from being perfect—
it comes from knowing who you are,
from embracing your flaws,
***from standing in your truth,* unshaken.**
Her birthright isn't just strength—
it's the freedom to love fully,
to heal deeply,
to rise continuously.
She is enough,
has always been enough.
And every time she breathes,
she declares to the universe:
"I am here,
I am whole,
and I am unstoppable."

To the Life We Build

She don't talk to God like they taught her—
nah, her prayers echo through kitchens,
where the clink of dishes meets whispered wishes.
She speaks not in hope, but in certainty,
her words an unshakable decree:
"We don't wait for what's deserved;
we create what's ours."

That's how she raises her baby—
not just on love,
but on the truth that's been tucked beneath her skin
for generations.

"We don't ask,"
she says, pressing her lips to a soft forehead,
"we take what's been owed to us."

She ain't raising no fragile heart;
this child is steel wrapped in velvet,
the kind of strength that comes easy,
like the sun rising,
like the moon pulling tides.

Her hands are calloused, but full of tenderness,
holding what the world might break,
but won't—
not on her watch.

"You're more than they'll ever see,"
she whispers,
"more than their eyes could ever hold."

Beneath Her Cracked Armor She Blooms

She plants dreams in the child's spirit,
waters them with words full of promise,
letting them grow in the cracks where doubt tried to live.
"They won't be ready for you,"
she says with a smile,
"but that's not your concern.
You've got greatness written in your bones,
a future carved out of stardust."

Her voice carries weight,
turning silence into something sacred.
She knows the world doesn't make room for those like her,
like her baby,
but that's fine—
they'll create their own universe.

There's no hesitation in her tone,
just certainty.
No need to ask,
no waiting for anyone else's time.

She sees her child, not as fragile,
but as fire—
a force that can't be contained.
"You don't need to fit,"
she tells them,
**"you were born to stand out,
to blaze a path where no road existed before."**

No small steps, no shrinking,
this baby was born for more.
She speaks in rhythms only the ancestors know,
every syllable planting new worlds
beneath the surface of her child's skin.

She don't ask for favors—
she commands what's hers,
the life her child will lead,

Beneath Her Cracked Armor She Blooms

the love they'll carry.
She raises them in joy,
not fear,
though she's seen too much
to pretend this world isn't waiting.

But that's why she speaks life into every corner,
carves out space with her words,
tells her child what they'll own,
what they'll conquer.

"We don't just survive."
Her voice is full of conviction.
**"We rise above it,
claim what's meant for us,
rewrite everything they said we couldn't touch."**

She knows what it's like to be overlooked,
so she raises this child to demand the world's gaze,
to walk with certainty,
no matter the odds.

She builds with her tongue,
weaving futures from promises,
dreams that sparkle in the dark
where the world would never expect light.
But she knows how to create light,
knows how to make something out of nothing.

Her baby?
That child will carry that same magic.

She lays a foundation with every step she takes,
setting her own path,
making sure her child won't follow—
but lead.

"You're destined for more,"
she whispers,
her words a melody only her baby knows.
"You're walking in spaces they never thought you'd see."

Her child's eyes are bright,
reflecting all the dreams she's spoken into existence.
No room for doubt here,
no space for fear.

She speaks, not with hope,
but with certainty—
"We're not waiting for life to open its doors.
We'll build our own kingdom,
claim every corner they left in shadow."

This isn't about surviving—
it's about **reclaiming, rebuilding,**
and rising.

Her child will walk in a world
that learns to bow,
not because it was demanded,
but because it was always meant to.

"The future is yours,"
she says with a smile,
because she knows.
She's seen it,
felt it,
spoken it into being.

Beneath Her Cracked Armor She Blooms

Beads and Bows

These beads ain't just beads—
they're echoes of **queens**,
remnants of **crowns** that once sat
high on the heads of **warrior** women
whose names they tried to bury in the dirt.
You think those bows are just ribbons?
                They're the **flags of a legacy**

                              tied at the end of your braids,

a reminder of the royalty stitched into your scalp.
Cornrows?
Those are maps,
lines drawn by hands that knew survival was more than skin deep.
They tell you it was just hair,
but those twists held secrets—
roads to freedom,
routes hidden in plain sight,
a resistance written in rows too neat to question.
Your hair—
it carries the story of escape,
of women who braided pathways to freedom
while the overseer's back was turned.
They didn't just braid hair;
                they braided hope,
              they twisted dreams into your roots,
each plait a promise that the road to liberation
was closer than they thought.

And those beads,
clacking like prayers in the wind,
aren't just decoration.
They're the songs of your **foremothers,**
their voices rattling in the rhythm of your steps.
Every time they click,
they're calling out to the **queens** who wore them first,

who strutted through palaces with heads held high,
the same way you do
walking down the block.
You were crowned before you even knew it.

Those Saturday mornings between your mama's knees,
she wasn't just doing your hair—
she was preparing you,
anointing you with the power of those who came before.
With every tug, every twist,
she was reminding you
that you come from women who carried nations on their heads
and freedom in their hands.

Bows at the ends of your braids,
not just to make you pretty,
but to tie you back to those who fought for your right
to walk this earth,
unapologetic,
unbowed.

Your scalp carries history.
Your braids are blueprints,
each part a direction,
each twist a step toward something bigger than you.

So when you walk,

let those beads rattle,

let them sing the songs of your ancestors,

let the world hear what they tried to silence.

This is for the girls who know

that their hair is not just hair—

it's a map,

it's a crown,

it's a battle cry.

<u>You carry the weight of queens,</u>

<u>of mothers who fought and never faltered.</u>

Walk with your head high,

let the beads be your anthem,

let the bows remind you that you were born

from the same blood as those who refused to be broken.

You, little **Black girl,**

are more than they will ever understand.

Your hair carries roads to freedom,

and your soul carries the strength

of women who dared to dream beyond the chains.

Pity Patters

I remember that day
    like a verdict dropped,
Mama storming in,
    no warning shot.
Uncle's laugh still hanging in the air,
me in his lap, talking like I didn't have a care.
    I hadn't seen him in years,
    his pockets full of dollars that felt like dreams,
and I was basking in it,
    letting the moment stretch longer than it seemed.

But Mama,
she cut through it,
    her voice sharp as truth,
    like she had seen something I couldn't.
    "Motherfucker, you lost your mind?
    Don't you ever let this daughter of mine
    sit between your legs,
    like that's alright."
She snatched me so fast,
    the room didn't even know how to breathe right.

Uncle's face, a mix of confusion and pride cracked.
He never saw it coming,
    didn't know what to say back.
But Mama wasn't talking to his feelings—
    she was speaking facts,
    laying down law like she'd seen the future.
And maybe she had,
    because she knew better than to trust the past.

It wasn't about him,

Beneath Her Cracked Armor She Blooms

but about what men do
    when lines blur
    and intentions twist in ways nobody wants to speak of.
    "It's never the stranger that puts us in danger,"
    she'd say,
    "It's the ones we know,
    the ones too close,
    the ones we trust until the trust gets broke."

 She called them pity patters—
    men whose hands wander too far,
    who leave marks too deep to see,
but you feel them—
    forever.
It's not rare, Mama knew—
93% of child victims know their abusers,
    most of them men who wear smiles like armor,
    men you never suspect,
    until the trust they broke leaves you wrecked.

I was too young to get it then,
    didn't know the weight behind her eyes,
    the history stitched into her skin.
But now,
    with my own daughter,
    my own son,
I feel that knowledge creeping up my spine—
    the kind that makes you cautious,
    the kind that makes you firm
    when the world is soft and dangerous.

Mama wasn't just mad,
    she was right.
She wasn't here for appearances,
    she was here to fight
    for the safety I didn't even know I needed.
    She understood the difference between a smile and a threat,

between a hug and hands that wander
into territory, they shouldn't forget.

And now, I get it.
    I understand why she didn't flinch,
      why she didn't care if Uncle's pride took a hit,
because she wasn't in the business of saving feelings—
    she was in the business of saving me.
She had lived enough life to know
    that innocence is fragile,
    and men—
    even good ones—
    sometimes don't know when to let go.

But not all men are like that.
    Uncle wasn't one of them.
He never touched me,
    never crossed that line,
and now with his own daughter,
    I think he understands it too.
Understands why Mama didn't leave room for doubt,
    why protection came first—
    above feelings, above family ties.
It was never about trust,
    it was about making sure no harm could slip in,
    about guarding the ones you love
    before danger even gets a chance.

It's strange how time catches up with you.
How what felt like overreaction then
    feels like protection now.
I see what she saw.
I've heard the stories,
how 1 in 9 girls,
    and 1 in 53 boys
    will face what we don't want to say out loud.
The hands that take without asking,
    the lines crossed without a sound.

Beneath Her Cracked Armor She Blooms

But not me.
    Not mine.
Mama raised me to speak,
    to defend before the line gets blurred,
    to know that no one's touch is worth the cost
    of staying quiet.
And now I pass that down,
    to my own—
    because pity patters don't wear labels,
    they hide in plain sight,
    in places where love gets confused
    and trust gets twisted just right.

So, I thank you, Mama,
    for seeing what I couldn't,
for showing me what it means
    to protect before the damage is done.
I carry your lessons like armor now,
    and I won't let anyone
    forget what you taught me.
Because once you know,
    there's no going back.

Tough Love

She never said it softly,
love didn't roll off her tongue like sugar—
it hit hard, like a warning,
like a lesson you had to learn before the world taught it the wrong way.

Her love was never cushioned in easy words,
but it was there,
always there,
wrapped tight in the way she said,
"No, you can't go outside,"
or **"Don't let the streetlights catch you."**
She wasn't raising a daughter for fun,
she was raising a daughter for survival.

In a world that sees Black girls like her
as grown before their time,
as loud before they've even spoken,
she had to make sure her daughter knew the difference
between being seen and being a target.

She didn't have time for softness—
not when the world outside their door wasn't built for girls like her,
not when the news spoke the names of Black women
like a eulogy,
another name lost,
another name forgotten.

She saw her daughter's beauty
but taught her how to wear it like armor,

Beneath Her Cracked Armor She Blooms

because beauty alone wouldn't save her from a world
that sees her as less.

"Don't trust too easy,"
she'd say,
while pulling tight on her daughter's braids,
fingers working like she was weaving protection into every strand.
**"Not everyone's your friend.
Not everyone's got love for you."**

She wasn't cold,
but she was cautious,
and her love came with a warning label:
**"Handle this world carefully.
It wasn't made for girls like us to rise."**

Her daughter would look at her,
confused sometimes,
wondering why love couldn't feel light,
why it had to come with a side of fear.
But that's the thing—
she was trying to keep her alive,
in a place that wants Black girls to disappear.

In every "no,"
there was a "yes" to something deeper—
a yes to living another day,
to coming home safe,
to making it through without falling into the traps
laid out by a system that never cared to see you win.

She didn't explain all the time,
didn't have to.
The lessons were loud enough
in the way she raised her voice
when her daughter rolled her eyes,
or tried to argue her way into spaces
her mother knew were not meant for her.

Beneath Her Cracked Armor She Blooms

**"You think I don't know?
I was you once,
walking into rooms thinking the world owed me kindness.
It doesn't."**

She never said, **"I love you"** the way TV moms did,
but her daughter knew—
it was in the way she wouldn't let her leave the house
without knowing how to hold her head high,
how to walk into a room without shrinking.

It was in the way she stayed up late
waiting for her to come home,
when the world outside was too quick to swallow Black girls whole.

Tough love,
hard love,
wasn't easy,
but it was necessary.
She was making sure her daughter didn't get lost
in a world that expects her to fold,
to lose herself,
to forget who she is.

This mother,
she didn't have the luxury of softness.
Not when her daughter's life was on the line.
She loved her fiercely,
loved her like steel,
because that's what the world would test her with—
and she wanted her daughter to come out stronger,
wanted her daughter to know,
that in this world,
being soft could get you broken.

So she built her tough,
but she built her right.
With love that could withstand the storm,

Beneath Her Cracked Armor She Blooms

love that didn't crumble under pressure,
love that would last longer than any sweet words
whispered too softly to survive.

The Way, They See Us

They tell us we're grown before we even know what grown means.
Too fast, they say,
Like womanhood wasn't placed on our backs
while we were still learning Double Dutch.
Like the curves, we didn't ask for
made us guilty of crimes we didn't commit.
From the start, they saw us not as kids,
but something to be consumed—
our skin rich with history,
yet all they saw were bodies.
Just hips and lips,
ripe for the taking before we even knew what that meant.
They tell us, "Cover up,"
like it's our fault their eyes linger too long,
like our Blackness alone made us too much.
They call us "fast,"
but what's fast about a child just trying to live
in a world that takes more than it gives?

At ten, they told me I was "too developed,"
like my body sent invitations I never wrote.
At twelve, they said I was **"asking for it,"**
as if the stares from grown men were my doing.
At fifteen, they looked at me with hunger,
the kind that made me want to erase the curves,
peel back my skin and start over.

We've been sexualized since birth,

Beneath Her Cracked Armor She Blooms

turned to objects before we found our truth.
They saw women when we were still girls,
then wonder why we walk through this world
with our guards up high,
ready for war,
afraid to cry.
They said, "Don't wear that,"
"Don't walk there."
"Don't laugh too loud, don't smile too much."
Like the harm done to us was ours to carry,
like we weren't just girls,
trying to be free.

And nobody warned us.
Nobody said our bodies would be seen as property,
that innocence would be stripped
and we'd be blamed for the theft.
Nobody told us being Black and a girl
meant growing up twice as fast,
because this world would rather devour us
than protect us.

The truth is,
we were sexualized before we even knew what sex was.
Our childhoods were cut short
by eyes that lingered too long,
by whispers, touches, and the weight of expectations
that we were always "strong enough" to bear.
But why did we have to bear it at all?

They told us to be quiet,
to stop drawing attention,
as if our Blackness wasn't already a spotlight.
But we are not the shame they tried to drape over our shoulders.
We are not the labels built around our bodies.

Beneath Her Cracked Armor She Blooms

We were girls,
and we deserved childhood, not objectification.
We are voices that deserve to be heard,
and now, we speak.
We tell our stories unashamed,
wearing this skin like the crown it is.

This body is not for their consumption.
This voice will not be silenced.
And this truth—
it will no longer be hidden

FITTING IN

Fitting in—
it's a story Black girls know too well,
trying to blend in,
but your skin tells tales louder than whispers in the hallway.

Your curls, thick like roots,
reach toward the sky,
pulling history from the air,
but the world keeps trying to shrink you,
to make you smaller,
make you quiet.

It's walking through halls
where eyes follow,
where laughter stops,
and you feel the weight of your ancestors
sitting on your shoulders,
telling you to stand tall
even when the room wasn't made for you.

Fitting in becomes a game,
but it's rigged—
they don't see you for the queen you are,
they don't hear the rhythm in your steps.

Lunchtime's a battlefield.
Tables divided like lines carved in stone,

Beneath Her Cracked Armor She Blooms

and the seats—
they're more than just places to sit,
they're claims to belonging.

But you don't need their table—
your people have been building their own for generations.

The whispers say, "Be like us."
But they don't know,
they don't understand that you carry a crown,
Invisible but heavy.

It's not just about school.
Fitting in—
it's the world's way of saying,
"Don't be too much, don't stand too tall."

But Black girls know—
too much is what we were born to be.
We were never meant to fold ourselves into small spaces,
never meant to walk quietly
through a world that's been built on our backs.

And fitting in?
That's not the goal.
The world has been trying to fit Black girls
into boxes we were never made for.
We've always been bigger,
brighter,
louder than the spaces they try to put us in.

So, when they tell you to be quiet,
walk louder.
When they say fit in,

Beneath Her Cracked Armor She Blooms

build your own door.
You don't have to belong to their table
when you can create your own.

Because this isn't about finding a place in their world—
it's about remembering that this world
was never meant to hold all that Black girls carry.

We are the rhythm,
the sound that can't be silenced.
We are the roots
that refuse to be buried.

"First Pair of Heels"

They weren't just shoes, they were a passage,
a door I was meant to walk through.
Leather straps hugging my ankles,
heels raising me up,
whispering, "You've arrived."
Not at the end,
                but at the beginning of something new,
something with a different weight.

Mama handed them to me,
no words, just a glance,
like she'd been waiting for this moment too.
There was no ceremony,
just the quiet understanding that
I was crossing over.

The first step *wobbled,*
    not from fear,
        but from feeling the ground leave
            beneath my feet for the first time.
                I wasn't walking
anymore—
                I was stepping into a space
          where the air felt different,
        where the clicks of the heels echoed,
    and I knew
something had shifted.

        This was a rite.
           Not written in books,
            but in the way my posture changed,
            in the way my mother nodded,

Beneath Her Cracked Armor She Blooms

in the way I could feel the past meeting the present
in every step I took.

The heels weren't just for fashion—
they were for learning how to balance,
how to move through this world
a little higher,
a little taller than before.
Each click against the floor was a reminder—
you're not a child anymore.
                                        It is in the way my feet
hurt
                    after hours of standing—
that pain wasn't weakness,
it was proof of the journey.
A silent badge of growing up,
earned in quiet moments like this.
    I looked down at my feet,
at the heels that now felt like a part of me,
and I realized—
this is what rites of passage feel like.
Not fireworks,
not applause,
just a quiet shift in the way you stand,
in the way the world stands with you.
The heels didn't make me grown,
but they were the first step toward something more—
toward learning how to carry the weight of womanhood
without losing balance.

Dear Black Daughter of the World,

Let me tell you what I wish I had learned earlier,
before the world convinced me that my worth
was tied to their expectations,
before I handed over pieces of myself
to people who never knew what to do with them.

First, know this—
you owe nothing.
Not your time, your peace, your silence, or your body.
There are those who will try to box you in,
make you small,
because that's easier for them to understand.
But you?
You weren't built to fit into their boxes.
You were made to rise, to expand,
to take up space in a world that isn't always ready for you.

And don't waste your time trying to make them ready.
Love is not a currency you have to beg for.
If it doesn't come freely,
let it go.
Your time is too precious to give away
to anyone who doesn't recognize its value.
Cry when you need to—
tears are part of the process—
but remember who you are when you're done.
Wipe your face, stand tall, and keep moving.

There will be moments when you stumble,
when the weight of it all feels too heavy.

Beneath Her Cracked Armor She Blooms

That's okay.
Just don't let that weight become a burden
you carry for too long.
This world isn't going to wait for you—
there's no "right time."
Move now,
move with intention.
And if they aren't ready for what you bring?
That's their burden to carry, not yours.

I spent too long trying to be what everyone else needed,
trying to keep peace at my own expense.
But peace doesn't come from pleasing others—
it comes from protecting yourself,
from knowing when to say no,
and meaning it.
Guard your energy like gold,
because it is.

There will be regrets,
there always are.
But don't let them root you in place.
I wish I could go back
and tell the younger version of myself:
"You don't need anyone's permission
to be who you are.
You are more than enough—just as you are."

Trust that inner voice,
the one that's been speaking to you all along.
It knows what you need,
even when the world tries to drown it out.
Stop waiting to be chosen by others.
Choose yourself.

The world will overlook you,
if you let it.
So don't wait to be seen—

see yourself first.
Forget about their expectations.
Your power is in knowing who you are,
and claiming that, unapologetically.

One more thing—
peace is something you find within.
You won't discover it in places that are built on chaos.
Walk away from what no longer serves you,
no matter how hard it feels.
It will hurt,
but staying in places that break you
will hurt even more.

This life will challenge you,
test you in ways you never imagined.
But you are stronger than any test.
You come from a lineage of women
who survived, who thrived,
even when the odds were against them.
That strength runs through you, too.

So, love yourself fully.
Choose yourself first.
You are enough—always have been.
And no matter what the world tries to tell you,
you are more than worthy of all the love and peace you seek.

With all the lessons I had to learn the hard way,
The Woman Who's Walked That Path

Granny's Mac & Cheese and Fried Chicken

Granny didn't just cook,
    she **crafted.**
Every pot on the stove was an **offering,**
    every flick of her wrist was a **sermon.**

That mac and cheese?
    That was **gold,**
heavy like the lessons she never had to say out loud.
    Cheddar layered thick,
    but it wasn't the cheese that stuck—
    it was the **love,**
        baked into every corner,
    the kind that wraps around you
    like a warm Sunday afternoon.

Her fried chicken?
    That wasn't just food.
    That was **armor.**
Crispy skin seasoned with a history you could taste,
    fried in a pan that had seen more life than most people.

Granny didn't need to say **"I love you"** much,
    she let the chicken **speak** for her,
    let the crackle of that hot grease tell you
    she was **holding it down for you**—
even when the world was trying to take you apart.

See, Granny knew something about **feeding souls,**
    about filling you up from the inside out.
It wasn't just collards and cornbread—
    it was **legacy,**
    passed down in every spoonful.

Beneath Her Cracked Armor She Blooms

That mac and cheese could hush the noise in your mind,
    remind you that you were built from more than just struggle.
Each bite pulled you back to yourself,
    like she was saying,
"I see you. Don't let them take your fire."

The way she fried that chicken,
you knew it wasn't her first time in the kitchen,
and it damn sure wouldn't be the last.
    Seasoned to the bone,
like she'd been perfecting this since way before we even knew
how important it was to have something to fall back on—
something that would remind us where we come from.

Granny's hands knew **pain**,
but they also knew how to create **joy**,
    and that's what her food was—
    joy in the middle of all the mess.

A plate full of reminders that even when life tries to knock you down,
there's still something sweet on the other side of it.
    That mac and cheese—
it held us together when things felt too heavy,
    when the world was too loud,
    and we just needed something solid to hold onto.

And that chicken?
It was a love letter,
crispy and golden,
saying,
"You ain't gotta fight alone, baby. I'm here."

Because that's what Granny's food was—
    not just dinner,
but a declaration.
    A way of saying,
"Even when everything else falls apart,

**we still got this.
We still got each other."**

 And I swear,
that fried chicken and mac and cheese,
    it tasted like **home.**
Not just a place,
but a **feeling—**
    something rooted,
    something real.
    Something you could always come back to.

APPLES TREE ROOTS

They say the apple don't fall far from the tree,
And I guess they was talkin' 'bout Mama, you, and me.
Three generations of smiles that stretch for miles,
Same height, same voice—same style.
On the phone, they can't tell us apart,
But it's more than sound; we share the same scars on the heart.

It's love, though, the kind you feel in your bones,
The kind that knows how to cook a meal that tastes like home.
Hips that carry history, moves that speak truth,
And a mouth that stays ready with a smart-ass proof.
Intellect sharp as the edge of a knife,
Words that cut deep or heal depending on life.
We poets, baby, every single one,
Three generations of spinnin' words, we make life run.
And you got that gift too,
A lover of art, of music, of everything true.

Favor? Girl, you've been blessed since your first breath,
It's in your blood, like Mama's gumbo, passed down with finesse.
Like my hustle, like the fights we done won,
It's all yours, baby girl—you're second to none.
But that hustle, see, it's both gift and curse,
We know how to grind, make gold from dirt, but we thirst
For peace, for rest that we ain't learned yet.
We work to the bone, but we ain't learned to just sit.

Beneath Her Cracked Armor She Blooms

Baby, watch out for the weight that we carry,
More than love, there's trauma, be wary.
Addiction? It runs through veins like rivers wide,
So be careful what you reach for when life ain't on your side.
We wasn't taught to love ourselves first,
We chased validation in folks who couldn't quench our thirst.
You got that way with words, like me, like her,
But remember, it cuts both ways, can bless or burn.
It's power, but it's dangerous too,
If you ain't mindful, it'll turn on you.

And I'm sorry, baby, for being a mama at seventeen,
Still lost, still searching, trying to find what it means
To raise you while figuring out how to be me—
You needed more, and I own that fully.
I wasn't whole, and you deserved better,
But now you're a mother, so here's my letter:
Be better than I was, love harder, love deep,
But don't forget yourself, don't lose what's yours to keep.

Give your babies all the love you wished I gave,
And teach them what we never learned—how to be brave,
How to know they're enough, worthy from birth,
They ain't gotta prove nothin' to claim their worth.
You carry so much of me, of her, of the past,
But you're the best parts, the strength that will last.

I see your spirit, bright as the sun,
And I know you'll rise, baby, I know you'll run.
I'm proud of you, for all that you do,
And I'm sorry for where I fell short, too.
But I'm here now, cheering you through,
Break every cycle, build something new.

Beneath Her Cracked Armor She Blooms

Love deeper, live freer, be bold in your grace,
And never forget where you come from, your place.
We're behind you, every step of the way,
Baby girl, you're the future—go on, make your way.

Her Life, My Lesson

She prayed in whispers,
like God only heard women who knew how to bow their heads low.
Dreamed in silence,
because the world told her dreams didn't belong to Black girls
who worked too hard
and slept too little.
She had hands built for labor,
a back that carried the weight of everything—
but never her own worth.

Mama loved like the ocean—
deep, relentless,
but always crashing against shores
that never held her.
She gave until her hands were empty,
gave until her heart was threadbare,
patched up with promises she never received back.
But love?
She knew it in pieces,
in broken things,
in men who only stayed long enough to take
and in children who needed everything
but never knew how to give it back.

Her pain sat in her eyes,
heavy,
like she could feel the weight of generations pulling her under.
She never cried—
not in front of us.
She didn't have time for tears,

Beneath Her Cracked Armor She Blooms

not when there were bills to pay,
not when there were mouths to feed,
not when survival was a battle she fought alone.
Her silence was her shield,
but it cut deeper than any words she never spoke.

Mama's dreams died quietly,
in the space between raising children
and folding laundry,
in kitchens where she cooked meals she didn't have the
appetite to eat.
I saw it—
the way she looked at the sky like she was searching for a door
she forgot to walk through.
She used to write,
used to sing before her voice got drowned out
by the sound of life demanding more than she could give.

But love?
She never learned how to give it to herself.
She was too busy holding the world up on tired shoulders,
too busy praying for strength instead of rest,
too busy convincing herself that if she just kept going,
maybe one day, someone would love her the way she loved
them.

I watched her pour herself out,
watched her shrink,
watched her become a ghost of the woman she might've been
if she had known how to love herself first.
Her prayers were for us,
her children,
but I wonder if she ever whispered one for herself.

What did it teach me?
That love without boundaries is a war you can't win.
That giving until you're empty only leaves you hollow.

Beneath Her Cracked Armor She Blooms

I learned that the world won't save you,
and no man will ever fill the space you refuse to occupy.

She taught me sacrifice,
but she didn't teach me to say no.
She taught me to survive,
but not to live.
So I learned on my own—
learned to build myself up from the pieces she left behind,
learned that love doesn't mean bleeding for everyone else,
that my dreams don't have to die
just because hers did.

I watched my mama love everyone but herself,
and it taught me this:
I won't follow that path.
I won't live in the shadow of what could've been.
I'll take her prayers, her dreams,
her silence—
and turn them into something more.

HIS HATS, BOOTS, AND ABSENCE

My Step-Daddy's hats and boots told stories—
stories of showing up, even when his bones were tired,
fighting to stay awake on the couch,
telling me, "I'm not tired, just resting my eyes,"
because he couldn't bear to miss a moment.
He laced up those boots every morning,
wore that hat low,
and came home with the weight of the world on his shoulders,
but still made time for me.
Still spun me around the kitchen floor,
boots scuffing the tiles,
while I laughed and held on tight.

But for every father that stays,
there's one that's gone—
gone before the first word,
gone before I ever knew what it meant to be held by a man
who didn't ask for anything in return.
Gone like air, like a promise that never meant to be kept.
You were supposed to be my first protector,
my first love,
but you left me searching for your shadow
in every man who came after.
I became the girl looking for answers
in faces that couldn't give them,
trying to fill the gap you left with every empty touch.

For the father who stayed,
there were boots by the door,

Beneath Her Cracked Armor She Blooms

worn and weary,
but never too tired to come home.
For the father who left,
there were only questions,
echoes in an empty house.
One taught me how to stand tall,
how to take up space,
how to love without fear.
The other taught me how to leave,
how to doubt,
how to wonder if I was ever worth staying for.

I look at the boots that carried Daddy home,
and I wonder what it feels like
to never have to question if you're wanted.
But then I remember—
there's also the hat that was never hung,
the chair that stayed empty,
and the silence that said more than any absence should.

For the father who stayed,
I learned strength.
I learned love wrapped in calloused hands,
hugs that held me together when the world tried to tear me apart.
For the father who left,
I learned resilience,
how to build walls around a heart that grew too used to goodbye.

But still, I'm standing.
For the father who showed me what it means to stay,

What They Took

She was soon to be turning twelve
when the world taught her what theft felt like.
It wasn't just a body they stole—
it was her sense of safety,
stripped in silence.
No screams, no bells
just hands that never asked for permission,
just eyes that saw her not as a child,
but as something to claim.
She learned quickly that the world had teeth,
and they weren't afraid to bite.
She stopped looking at herself in the mirror the same way,
started wearing her skin like a stranger—
too tight,
too exposed,
like it wasn't hers to live in anymore.
Nobody asked the right questions.
Nobody told her that when you're Black and a girl,
they never see you as young—
you're grown as soon as your body curves,
and nobody's listening to the parts of you
that are still soft, still learning how to be.
Her mama didn't know how to talk about it.
Nobody did.
She carried that silence like a stone in her chest,
heavier than the shame they handed her.
It wasn't her fault,
but she learned the world would make her feel like it was—
every side-eye, every whisper,
telling her to stay small,

Beneath Her Cracked Armor She Blooms

to not take up space,
because space was dangerous for girls like her.
At fifteen, she started to armor up—
not in steel, but in silence.
She let her walls speak for her.
Her smile turned sharp,
her eyes always watching,
reading the room before she ever walked in.
She wasn't naïve anymore;
the world had taught her too much
too soon.
By seventeen,
she had mastered the art of disappearing,
learned to fade into the background,
to avoid the gaze that made her feel
like prey again.
Every man's stare felt like a loaded gun,
and she was tired of dodging bullets
no one else could see.
But she wasn't just running—
she was learning.
Learning how to reclaim the pieces they'd taken.
Learning that what they stole
wasn't all she had to give.
Her body was hers again,
even if it took years for her to believe it.
She walked through the world with her chin up,
because she had to.
Because if she didn't,
the weight of it all would bury her.
She was learning to rewrite her own story,
to take the pen from the hands of those
who had tried to write her ending
before she even got to start.
She was growing into her womanhood,
not with the softness they expected,
but with the strength she had earned.
Every scar a line in her history,

every bruise a map to the places she'd escaped.
Her heart?
Still beating,
still hers,
still full of love,
even after everything.
She learned that survival wasn't just about breathing,
it was about choosing to live.
Choosing to wake up every day
and decide that what they took
wouldn't define her,
wouldn't be the last chapter in her story.
She was writing herself new every day,
with the ink of resilience,
with the language of forgiveness—
not for them,
but for herself.
Because the world is hard on Black girls.
It tells them to be strong,
but it never asks if they want to be.
She didn't ask for this weight,
but she carried it anyway,
and in carrying it,
she found a way to lighten it.
In reclaiming her body,
she reclaimed her voice,
and when she spoke,
it wasn't just for her—
it was for every Black girl
who had ever been silenced.

And in her silence, there was a roar.

My Mama Never Taught Me About Birds & the Bees

Mama never sat her down,
never spoke in hushed tones about love or lust,
about what happens when boys get too close,
or when the world tries to claim parts of you
before you're ready to give them.

She had to figure it out on her own,
like most Black girls do—
from whispers in hallways,
from music videos that made it look too easy,
from friends who knew as little as she did
but still spoke like they had the answers.

Her first lesson?
That curiosity gets you caught up,
and nobody tells you about the trap
until you're already in it.
She didn't know the difference
between a want and a need,
so she let someone else define it for her,
until she realized
that they never had her in mind
when they talked about the "birds and the bees."

They made it sound soft,
like love was something that fluttered,
something that felt like a breeze—
but she learned it hit harder,
left marks,
carved spaces into her heart
she didn't even know existed.

Beneath Her Cracked Armor She Blooms

Nobody warned her
about the shame that comes wrapped around desire,
about how the world sees Black girls as too grown
before they even learn what their bodies are for.

Nobody told her
that innocence is a luxury they don't let you keep,
that your curves get noticed before your smile,
and boys don't see you as somebody's daughter,
they just see what you've got.

She learned the hard way
that the world teaches you about your body
by taking pieces of it,
and that love,
the kind they sing about,
doesn't always feel like butterflies.
Sometimes it feels like something you're running from,
something you didn't ask for.

Mama never taught her about love.
She was too busy surviving
to teach her how to hold it,
how to keep it from slipping through her fingers.

So, she watched,
watched the world make decisions for her,
until one day she decided to make her own.

She learned that her body was hers
before it was anyone else's,
that pleasure wasn't a sin,
but the guilt they tried to hand her was.

She learned to love herself first,
in a world that never told her
she was allowed to.

She taught herself about the birds and the bees,
about how her body was more than just something to be wanted,
but something to be held, cherished,
respected in a way the world never did.

She learned how to rewrite the rules
they never gave her,
how to make space for her voice
in a story that was always hers to tell.

CHASING LOVE IN THE DARK

She grew up watching her mama
love men who never stayed,
and somewhere along the way,
she thought that was how it had to be—
that love came with pain,
that you had to beg for it,
or bleed for it,
because that's what she saw.

Nobody taught her what real love was supposed to feel like,
so she tried to find it anywhere she could.
She chased boys who didn't know her name,
boys who saw her curves but never her heart,
boys who took but never stayed long enough to give.

She didn't know her worth,
because nobody told her that she was more than just what she
gave away.
She thought love meant being needed,
so she poured herself into boys
who couldn't even hold a piece of her soul,
let alone the whole of her.

She thought maybe if she gave enough of herself,
he'd see her—
the girl who was still waiting for love that never came.
The one who had been left too many times,
by too many people
who were supposed to stay.
But boys like him?
They don't know how to love girls like her.

Beneath Her Cracked Armor She Blooms

Black girls don't get the fairy tales—
we get the heartbreaks,
we get the lessons in survival,
in how to carry the world on our backs
while pretending like it ain't too heavy.

She didn't have a daddy to show her what real love looked like,
                        so she clung to boys who reminded her
                              of everything she was missing.
                                  She wanted him to stay,
                                      but deep down,
          she knew he wasn't made to love her the way she needed.
She knew he was just another boy who couldn't see her pain.

                But she stayed, hoping,
          because Black girls are taught to hope
             even when hope feels like a lie.
        She stayed, giving him pieces of herself
             that she could never get back,
            thinking that maybe, just maybe,
             he'd love her enough to heal her.

But that's not how it works.
You can't heal what's broken inside of you
by giving yourself to people
who don't even know how to hold you.
And she was broken,
in places she didn't know how to name,
in ways that made her think
love was something you had to fight for,
something you had to suffer for.

                                  But now she's learning
                                  that love starts with her.
                      That no boy can fill the space
                    where her father should've been,
           where her mama's love wasn't enough to reach.
              She's learning that Black girls deserve more

> than just the pieces we're handed,
> that we don't have to settle
> for boys who can't love us whole.

She's learning that love isn't something you beg for.
It's something you build,
first in yourself,
and then with someone who sees you—
all of you.

Pieces Left Behind

They told her bodies were bridges,
but nobody warned her
about the toll.

She walked across too many,
thinking **love** was on the other side,
but all she found
were footprints
that didn't belong to her.

Statistics said she wasn't alone,
that **1 in 4** girls like her
had their **innocence stolen**
before they even knew what innocence meant.
But numbers don't ease the weight,
don't explain the hollow that grows
where trust used to live.

She became a lesson in **survival**,
learned how to give what was expected,
how to **hand over pieces**
before they were taken by force.
But there's a cost to giving too much—
the price is yourself.

She thought she could find wholeness
in men's hands,
but wholeness never came.

What did come were scars,
invisible but deep,

etched into her skin by every night
she spent trying to forget the first one.

Beneath Her Cracked Armor She Blooms

They said **90%** of survivors
know their abusers—
that fact haunted her like a ghost.
She thought if she could choose the next one,
it would hurt less.
It didn't.

Her journey became a cycle,
a search for control in places
where control was always slipping through her fingers.
She wasn't running toward love,
but away from pain.
And in the running,
she lost sight of what she was chasing.

By 18, she'd stopped counting,
because counting didn't heal.
It just reminded her
of how many pieces she'd scattered
along the way.

But healing isn't about what you've lost—
it's about what you reclaim.

70% of women who walk her path
never see therapy.
She didn't either.
She thought silence was strength,
thought coping was something you did in private.
But silence just made the cracks deeper.

She was **16** when the world first called her "fast."
But speed isn't the problem—
it's the direction.
She wasn't looking for lust;
she was looking for something **safe**,
something that felt like shelter.
But safety doesn't come in unfamiliar arms.

Beneath Her Cracked Armor She Blooms

Now, after years of empty rooms,
she knows her worth isn't in giving—
it's in keeping.
She's learned that nothing stolen defines her,
that no tally of nights spent forgetting
can erase the woman she's becoming.

This journey isn't about who didn't stay,
it's about learning
that staying for herself was always the goal.

She isn't a statistic anymore,
she's a survivor
rewriting the numbers

To The Boy Whose Mama Called My House

I thought I was grown back then,
passing notes like secrets in the hall, writing love letters in ink too heavy for a 12-year-old heart to hold. You remember?
We checked boxes like contracts; Do you like me? Yes, no, maybe?
I thought we had something real between the lockers and late-night calls, *67'd and whispered after midnight, praying my father wouldn't hear the click of him picking up the other line.

I joined teams I didn't care about, clubs I had no interest in—
just to sit next to you, just to feel grown. Smelling myself, like my daddy said. I was running wild in his eyes, but still his little girl, too young to know how fast I was flying into a storm.

I thought I knew love, but what did I know at twelve? Wrote you that letter, three pages of words I couldn't even say out loud— lyrics stolen from R. Kelly and Janet, talking 'bout "That's the way love goes," when I didn't know where it was headed.

I said I'd have your baby. Didn't even know what that meant, but I wrote it like a promise on lined paper. Thought I was so grown.

Then your mama found it. Read those words like a warning sign, like a red flag waving too close to her baby boy. She picked up the phone, called my house, called my father.

I'll never forget the night y'all came over. I was supposed to be at the fall formal, dressed up, smiling, but instead I was sitting in our family room, with your mom and mine, and my father's voice booming like thunder across the silence.

He made me sit there, made me read that letter out loud, each line more grown than I was, each word feeling heavier with your mama's eyes on me, with my father's disappointment in the room. I couldn't even get through it. I was embarrassed, but I didn't know what I was doing, didn't know why I was rushing to be something I wasn't.

You see, that summer before I was broken open, by something I couldn't name, by hands that shouldn't have touched, and it made me think I was ready for things I wasn't. I wanted to be grown because I thought that was how you survived.

But now, years later, I want to thank your mama. She saw something I didn't see. She protected you from words you weren't ready to read, protected me from a path I wasn't ready to walk. And now that I have a son of my own, I get it.

I get the love she had for you, the way she stepped in.
I didn't know it then, but she was protecting me, too.

So, to the boy whose mama I said snitched on me,

Thank your mama for me—

ROOTS THAT HOLD

In the quiet corners of her grandmother's house,
Secrets lingered like shadows,
Whispers of a past steeped in pain,
Where love was often masked by trauma,
And laughter danced on the edge of sorrow.
She learned early on—
Family doesn't always mean safety.
It was a bloodline of silent battles,
Of women who wore their pain like bullet proof vest,
Carrying burdens that should never have been theirs.

  Her mother, a strong woman forged in the fire,
    Taught her how to hide her clever—
 "Keep your chin up, don't let them see you break."
 But what they never spoke of were those long nights
  When tears flowed like rivers down tired cheeks,
 When the weight of unspoken words filled the air.
   They carried the ghosts of their mothers,
    The secrets of infidelities, addictions,
 And the broken cups spilling out dreams deferred.

         But this woman—
         She was different.
     She refused to let the past define her.
    With every heartbeat, she made a choice,
       To dig deep into her roots,

Beneath Her Cracked Armor She Blooms

To honor the struggles, but not be shackled by them.
She pulled the stories from the ground,
Wrapped them around her children like a warm blanket,
But this time, she added love—
The kind that didn't come with conditions,
The kind that held space for healing.

"Listen, my loves,
Our family has stories, but we don't have to carry the pain."
She taught them the truth,
That resilience isn't just about pushing through;
It's about grabbing hold to new heights, freedom, joy
doing what you truly love in life
They spoke openly, shared their fears,
Turned their scars into stars guiding them home.
No more secrets hidden beneath the floorboards,
No more shame whispering in the dark.

With every lesson, she planted seeds,
In gardens of hope and understanding,
Where laughter could bloom freely,
Where vulnerability was strength,
And love was a fierce, unyielding force.
She broke the cycle,
Not with bitterness, but with grace,
And her children learned to stand tall,
Roots reaching deep, branches stretching wide,
Grounded in the knowledge that they were enough.

Now, when they gather at the table,
Stories flow like wine, rich and sweet,
And the air is filled with laughter,
Not just the echoes of the past,
But the melody of a new beginning.

Beneath Her Cracked Armor She Blooms

They talk of dreams, of hopes, of love,
Unraveling the threads of history,
Weaving a tapestry of strength and resilience,
A legacy that will stand firm through storms.

So here she stands,
This woman, a bridge between what was and what will be,
Rooted in the strength of her ancestors,
But blossoming in the light of her choices.
And she knows, deep down,
That breaking the silence was her greatest act of love,
That her family's history is not a burden,
But the soil from which their future will grow

HER FIRST-BORN SON

She looks at him now,
a man standing tall,
but once, he was a baby in her arms,
and she was just a child herself.
She didn't know what it meant,
to raise a life when she was still figuring out her own.
A girl turned mother too soon,
lost in a world that never taught her how to love herself first.

She did what she knew—
followed the same path her mama had shown,
thinking maybe love would fill the gaps.
But love doesn't patch up wounds that run deep,
and he needed more than the broken pieces
she had to give.

She watched him grow,
eyes full of questions she couldn't answer.
Why wasn't she there when he needed her most?
Why did the love feel distant,
like something just out of reach?
She had tried, she did—
but trying isn't enough
when you're lost in your own struggle,
fighting to be whole.

Her firstborn, her son,
he felt the weight of her silence,
felt the gaps she couldn't fill.
She gave what she had,

Beneath Her Cracked Armor She Blooms

but what she had wasn't enough
to erase the pain of being a mother
still learning how to stand on her own.

She carried the same scars her mama did,
repeating the same steps in a cycle she didn't know how to break.
A Black girl, lost, like so many before her—
thinking she could fix it with love
but finding out love needs more than heart.
It needs healing,
it needs hands that know how to hold without breaking.

She was too young to understand that then,
and now, she sees it in his eyes—
the questions, the hurt, the spaces she left behind.
He wonders why she didn't stay,
why she couldn't be strong enough,
steady enough to catch him when he fell.
But she was falling too.

She looks at him now,
and sees the man he's becoming,
despite the cracks she left.
He's strong in ways she never taught him,
and that's the part that cuts deep—
knowing he found his way without her,
even when she should have been his guide.

She whispers an apology into the air,
not loud enough for him to hear,
but enough to let it breathe—
a sorry for the mistakes she made,

Beneath Her Cracked Armor She Blooms

for the love she tried to give
but didn't know how to offer whole.

He needed a mother,
and she was still a girl,
learning what it meant to be more.
But the world doesn't stop for growing pains,
and she couldn't stop the cycle
from spinning him into her story,
one written long before he arrived.

But he was always loved,
even when she didn't know how to show it right.
And now, she sees him—
not just as her son,
but as a reflection of everything she tried to be
and everything she missed along the way.

"Raising Him in a World Not Built for Him"

She tells him, *"Baby, they won't always see your heart,*
    won't always look beyond your skin,
but *I need you to know,*
    you are more than what they think.
More *than the box they'll try to put you in."*

He asks about his father sometimes,
    and she holds her breath,
searching for answers
    that don't sting.
She tells *him that being a man*
    isn't just about strength,
it's *about kindness,*
    about showing up,
    about knowing when to stay.
But deep down, she's still learning,
    still figuring out
how to be both mother and father,
how to give him what she never had.

She's healing,
    but healing is messy,
and some days she wonders if she's doing enough.
    How can she teach him to stand tall,
when she's spent so many years
    learning not to fall?

He's **growing**,
    taller every day,
and she's scared.
    Scared of the day the world sees him as a man,
when to her,

Beneath Her Cracked Armor She Blooms

he'll always be her boy.
How do you tell an 11-year-old
    that the world isn't kind,
that it'll try to break him
    just because of who he is?

So she prays,
    prays that she's enough,
that love will be enough
    to cover the cracks in their foundation.
Prays that her mistakes
    won't become his,
that he'll learn to rise
    even when the world tries to pull him down.

She can't teach him to be a man,
    but she can teach him to be kind,
to walk with his head high,
    even when the world tries to make him small.
She can teach him that being strong
    isn't about fists,
it's about knowing when to use your voice,
    about knowing your worth
    when the world tells you otherwise.

And though she can't protect him
    from everything,
she wraps him in love,
    a shield only a mother could give.
She teaches him to fight—
    not with his hands,
but with his heart

Mirror- Mirror

I stand here, face to face,
with the only truth I can't erase.
The mirror doesn't blink, it don't flinch,
just reflects every scar,
every line,
every bruise life carved into my skin.

I'm standing with the weight of my story,
bare, exposed—
No more hiding behind ghosts I swore I buried.
They haunt me, still lingering in the back of my mind,
mistakes I can't shake,
regrets I can't leave behind.

"Who are you?" I ask the woman who stares back,
bags beneath her eyes, heavy with nights spent fighting,
wars nobody else could see.
She's been her own worst enemy more times than she'd like to admit.
Yet here she stands, her reflection demanding to be felt.

Mirror work ain't for the faint-hearted.
This ain't just gazing—
it's a reckoning.
I face I see every time I let them take
a piece of me,
without a fight,
and swallowed my own worth
like it was easier to choke than scream.

I feel the weight of every vice,
every addiction I wore like chains,

Beneath Her Cracked Armor She Blooms

and the voices that held me captive,
locked in a cell I built myself.

But still, I stand, eye to eye,
refusing to look away this time.

"You survived," I say,
and I swear, something in her shifts—
her bones, her breath, they sway.

"You made it through nights that stretched forever,
through days when breathing
felt like drowning."

I see your strength now—
not in muscle, not in the false armor you wore,
but in the scars, in the way you rebuilt yourself,
piece by piece,
when the world tried to tear you apart.

She's not perfect—
never was, never will be.
But there's power in her imperfections,
every crack is a lesson,
every break is a scar she turned into steel.

Today, I honor her for every fight—
lost and won.
For every time she let the darkness take control,
and for every time she found the strength
to crawl back from the edge.

She rose from her own ashes,
built something out of the wreckage.

I forgive her for the nights she reached
for comfort in all the wrong places.
I forgive her for the times she gave in,

Beneath Her Cracked Armor She Blooms

when she let the demons in,
when she doubted herself,
thought she wasn't enough.

But now I see her, clearly—
the beauty in her pain,
the power in her healing.
She took what was shattered,
and made it whole.

Today, I tell her:
"You are the warrior, the storm, the calm.
You rebuild, you reclaim,
you break the chains they tried to bind you with.
You hold the fire they swore would burn you down,
but here you are—standing,
unbroken."

I don't need her to smile,
I just need her to know:
You Are Enough.
You always were.
You always will be

Beneath Her Cracked Armor She Blooms

CHASING LOVE IN THE DARK"

She grew up watching her mama
love men who never stayed,
and somewhere along the way,
she thought that was how it had to be—
that love came with pain,
that you had to beg for it,
or bleed for it,
because that's what she saw.

Nobody taught her what real love was supposed to feel like,
so she tried to find it anywhere she could.
She chased boys who didn't know her name,
boys who saw her curves but never her heart,
boys who took but never stayed long enough to give.

She didn't know her worth,
because nobody told her that she was more than just what she gave away.
She thought love meant being needed,
so she poured herself into boys
who couldn't even hold a piece of her soul,
let alone the whole of her.

She thought maybe if she gave enough of herself,
he'd see her—
the girl who was still waiting for love that never came.
The one who had been left too many times,
by too many people
who were supposed to stay.
But boys like him?
They don't know how to love girls like her.

Beneath Her Cracked Armor She Blooms

Black girls don't get the fairy tales—
we get the heartbreaks,
we get the lessons in survival,
in how to carry the world on our backs
while pretending like it ain't too heavy.

She didn't have a daddy to show her what real love looked like,
so she clung to boys who reminded her
of everything she was missing.
She wanted him to stay,
but deep down,
she knew he wasn't made to love her the way she needed.
She knew he was just another boy who couldn't see her pain.

But she stayed, hoping,
because Black girls are taught to hope
even when hope feels like a lie.
She stayed, giving him pieces of herself
that she could never get back,
thinking that maybe, just maybe,
he'd love her enough to heal her.

But that's not how it works.
You can't heal what's broken inside of you
by giving yourself to people
who don't even know how to hold you.
And she was broken,
in places she didn't know how to name,
in ways that made her think
love was something you had to fight for,
something you had to suffer for.

He couldn't love her,
because he didn't know how to love himself.
But she didn't know that either,
so she kept chasing him—
chasing love like it was something
she had to find outside of herself.

Beneath Her Cracked Armor She Blooms

But now she's learning
that love starts with her.
That no boy can fill the space
where her father should've been,
where her mama's love wasn't enough to reach.
She's learning that Black girls deserve more
than just the pieces we're handed,
that we don't have to settle
for boys who can't love us whole.

She's learning that love isn't something you beg for.
It's something you build,
first in yourself,
and then with someone who sees you—
all of you.

ROADMAPS IN MY REARVIEW

It starts slow,
like driving in the dark,
on a road, you don't know,
barely seeing two feet ahead,
hands gripping tight,
wondering where you're supposed to go.

They don't tell you self-love looks like this—
like confusion,
like staring at mirrors and asking,
"Who am I without them?"

At first, it's shaky,
you treat it like a task,
something to fix, something to craft.
You pour into your skin, your hair,
thinking if you look right,
you'll feel right.
But sis, let me say—
that's just the start.
It's the primer, not the art.

You stand there, looking for signs,
thinking love will show up
when someone else does,
but love's no passenger.
It's you, behind the wheel,
making U-turns when life sends you wrong.

Beneath Her Cracked Armor She Blooms

It's smiling when it's just you
and your thoughts,
saying "I'm enough,"
not just because it sounds tough,
but because you've sat in silence long enough
to know your worth.

Then comes the phase
where you try to fill the gaps—
throw yourself into distractions,
dates that feel like detours,
hoping their touch is the spark
you've been waiting for.

But deep down, you know—
they're just pit stops.

Real love?
It starts with you,
and you've been avoiding your own heart
for too long.

At some point, you'll hit a wall,
realize self-love ain't just spa days
or cute Instagram quotes.
It's sitting in your silence,
listening to the parts that ache,
the ones that laugh too loud,
cry too late.

It's learning to love those pieces,
even when they don't fit anyone's frame
but yours.

Beneath Her Cracked Armor She Blooms

And when you reach that place?
It's freedom.

It's waking up
without checking your phone,
not waiting on a text to feel whole.
It's brewing your coffee
just how you like it,
because you know your flavor,
and you don't ask anyone to change it.

You start to walk different.
Not because someone said you're beautiful,
but because you saw it,
finally, for yourself.

You laugh at jokes you made,
dance in the kitchen,
finding rhythm in your own company.

That's the kind of love
that doesn't fade
when someone walks away.

And let's be real—
it's not a straight line.

Some days, you'll still doubt,
you'll look at your bed
and wish it was warmer,
but those days?
They don't define you anymore.

Beneath Her Cracked Armor She Blooms

You've built a home inside yourself,
one that feels like peace,
even when it's quiet.

And when love comes again,
you'll welcome it,
but you won't need it
to be whole.

You'll open the door,
but the locks are yours,
and you won't hand over the keys
just because they asked nice.

This journey?
It's yours—
no map, no GPS, no co-pilot.
It's you, navigating curves,
finding joy in the detours,
and knowing,
no matter where you end up,
you are your destination.

MADE FOR THE STORM

I've known the storm since I was young,
felt its breath heavy on my neck,
heard it whisper my name like a challenge.
Seen the skies fill with darkness, but I don't blink,
because this is where I was born—
in the eye of the commotion, where peace feels foreign,
and staying alive is the only thing I've ever trusted.

When the rain falls, it doesn't ask for permission,
it just comes, heavy and unrelenting,
and I don't run from it.
I stand still, and I let it wash all over me,
each drop like a reminder of all the shit I've faced,
of the woman I've had to become.
I ain't never the one to shrink in the wind.
I let it howl,
let it tear through me,
because I'm not fragile bitch!
I was made for this.

I don't fear the lightning;
I raise my head to the sky,
dare it to strike,
because I know—
I was built for this battle.
Born into it, raised by it,
the storm is mine.

I wear its marks like a crown,
each struggle like a jewel set in place.
I don't flinch when the skies tear open,
don't run when the thunder shakes the ground.

Beneath Her Cracked Armor She Blooms

I stand firm,
rooted like the trees that bend but don't break,
because I've learned that the storm doesn't destroy me—
it shapes me.
It turns me into something stronger,
something unshakable,
and I rise,
not in spite of it,
but because of it.

I used to think calm was where I belonged,
but now I know—
I was never meant to live in the quiet.
I was born for the roar,
for the nights when the winds rage
and nothing feels certain.
That's when I'm at my best,
when the world feels too heavy
 and I'm still here, standing.

So let it come,
let it rain, let it fall, let it break,
because I'll be here when it clears,
STILL STANDING,
stronger than the storm ever imagined.
This is my story,
this is my fight,
and the storm?
It's just the soundtrack to my everyday norm.

NEW SKIN

                You ever see a snake shed its skin?
     It leaves behind what no longer fits,
       slipping out of the old,
not out of want,
       but out of necessity.

        That's where I am now.
          No grand speeches,
               no sparks in the air,
      just the quiet truth
that the life I've been living
has grown too tight—
      like a cicada cracking free from its shell.

      I wore my past like layers,
believing I had to carry it forever.
                     But this new skin?
             It's lighter now,
      less burdened,
ready to let go of the weight.

You ever see a tree let go of its leaves,
     how it releases what's no longer needed?
I'm learning to do that—
     to drop what's finished,
and make room for what's next.

     This new skin doesn't seek applause,
doesn't need validation.
     It's like a butterfly leaving behind the cocoon—
     I've outgrown the spaces
I thought were my safety.

Beneath Her Cracked Armor She Blooms

I used to hold back,
        afraid of shedding too much,
        scared of what I might lose.
           But now I see—
                letting go isn't losing.
                The old skin had its season,
                      but it's time to grow out of it.

            This isn't about being tough—
      it's about finding freedom again.
I no longer carry the weight of silence,
don't shrink into the shadows
        of what I used to be.

You ever watch a snake slide away,
      lighter, freer?
That's what this feels like.

        Now I walk in this new skin,
            not because I have too,
                but because I want to.
            I'm not running toward a destination—
      I'm simply stepping forward,
unafraid of what I might shed next.

THE COLOR OF MY VOICE"

Blue
My voice began in blue—
not the bright cerulean of open skies,
but the deep, midnight hue,
where whispers hover just above silence.
It was the color of held breath,
of words pressed to the edge of my tongue
but never fully released.
Blue was stillness,
a voice learning its place in a world
that didn't ask for it.
The sound of oceans before they remember to crash.

Yellow
Then it softened into yellow,
full of the curiosity of new beginnings,
like sunbeams peeking through blinds—
small glimpses of brightness,
warm but unsure.
It was light-hearted but with depth,
a voice that tiptoed into spaces,
feeling for its place.
Yellow questioned,
reached out but pulled back just the same,
as if asking, "Am I enough to fill this room?"

Green
Next, green—
lush and alive,
like vines creeping up walls.
It wasn't loud, but steady,
the color of becoming,

growing even in places where there seemed to be no soil.
Green spoke of potential,
of resilience you don't always see coming,
pushing upward toward something greater,
reaching for the sun,
even when it wasn't sure what lay beyond the branches.

Red
Then came red,
bold and unapologetic—
the voice that no longer whispered.
It was fire on the horizon,
a sunrise you couldn't ignore.
Red was the language of passion,
a flame that said, "I am here, and I will not wait for permission."
It tore through expectations,
refusing to linger in shadows,
speaking truths that weren't always kind,
but necessary.
This was my revolution,
an eruption from the depths of a soul
that had been too quiet for too long.

Orange
After the fire, there was orange,
a warm ember,
not as wild but with a glow that lasted.
Orange was calm intensity,
the kind of voice that could stand in its fullness,
no longer rushed.
It was the harvest after the burning,
the wisdom gathered from the flame,
carried forward in the heat of its lessons.
Orange lingered—
the glow that stayed long after the sun had dipped below the horizon.

Purple
Purple came next—
regal, deep, the voice of knowing.
It didn't announce itself loudly,
but its presence shifted the air.
Purple was the sound of confidence without demand,
a voice seated on a throne built from experience.
It carried the weight of every truth,
spoken and unspoken,
a silent authority that spoke volumes
without raising its tone.
Purple was the voice of wisdom collected over years,
a quiet storm,
gathering all it had learned.

Silver
Then silver—
sharp as moonlight cutting through the night,
clear, distinct,
the voice of precision.
It wasn't harsh,
but it cut through the fog of uncertainty,
a reflection of clarity,
shimmering in the dark.
Silver didn't ask questions;
it answered them.
It was the voice of decisions made,
of paths chosen,
with an understanding
that not everything had to be explained.

Gold
Now, my voice is gold—
not the glitter of show,
but the quiet brilliance that holds itself,
precious and unyielding.
Gold is the sound of value—
unquestioned, known,

an understanding that shines from within,
radiating without the need for recognition.
It holds space,
commands without force.
Gold is timeless,
the voice of self-assurance,
knowing that it never needed to seek approval
because its worth was always intrinsic.

Black
And sometimes, my voice is black—
not darkness,
but the fullness of all colors combined,
a deep, quiet power.
Black is the voice that absorbs,
that listens,
that carries history and future in one breath.
It doesn't speak unless necessary,
but when it does,
it's like a drumbeat—
steady, profound, undeniable.
Black holds the universe in its silence,
an echo of everything
that's been said and all that will be.

SAY IT AGAIN

You said it wrong again—
tripped over my name like it wasn't carved from gold,
like it didn't carry generations in every syllable.
But I'm not here to teach you how to pronounce me.
I'm here to remind myself
that my name was never meant for your tongue to twist.

This name ain't just letters—
it's legacy.
My mama gave it breath,
and her mama before her gave it roots.
Every mispronunciation is a reminder
that you don't know where I come from.
But I do.

My name—
it's not yours to water down,
to chop up,
to make easier for your mouth.
I was never meant to be easy.

Say it right or don't say it at all,
because my name,
it's the drumbeat of my people,
the rhythm of resilience.
You don't get to claim it,
you don't get to reshape it.
It's mine.

Every time you butcher it,
I reclaim it,
putting it back together
like my ancestors pieced together songs
when they had no language but survival.

Beneath Her Cracked Armor She Blooms

My name ain't a question mark.
It's an exclamation.
It's power stitched into sound.
And every time you try to stumble over it,
I rise,
knowing it was never meant to fit in your mouth.
It was meant to stand out,
sharp

Ode to Old School

Remember Saturday mornings,
when the smell of bacon meant it was time to wake?
    Not to cartoons,
    but to Anita Baker, Al Green,
    and Mama hummin' while she cleaned the whole house.
Windows open, breeze blowin',
    And that Pine-Sol smell? It hit different.

That was the soundtrack to our lives,
The kind of music that made you feel something,
    Made you believe in love,
    Even when you didn't know what love was yet.

Let's talk about those trips to the beauty salon,
    Sitting between Auntie's knees,
      Getting your hair braided tight enough to make you tear,
    But you stayed still 'cause you knew—
Those cornrows were gonna be on point by the end.
Blue Magic on your scalp,
And when that hot comb hit the kitchen?
    You held your breath,
    Prayin' she didn't catch your ear.
But when you left that chair, girl,
    You felt brand new, ready for the world to cheer.

We were queens of Double Dutch,
    Jumpin' rope in the street with your girls,
    Rocking K-Swiss and jelly sandals,
    While hollering out the rhymes:
"Miss Mary Mack, Mack, Mack…"
    And when you weren't outside,

Beneath Her Cracked Armor She Blooms

You were inside, watchin' 106 & Park,
Waiting for your favorite music video to drop.

The joy when your song came on?
    It was like nothing else in the world mattered.
Remember summer cookouts,
    Cousins runnin' around,
    Old heads slappin' dominoes,
    And that one uncle always too loud but funny as hell?

Paper plates stacked with BBQ,
Mac and cheese so good it made you close your eyes.
    Ice pops drippin' down your wrist,
    While the grown folks told stories you wasn't supposed to hear,
    But you listened anyway,
    And laughed with your mouth full of secrets.

And don't get me started on the hair wraps at night,
    Making sure that press lasted all week,
    'Cause you knew you better not let that wrap slip.

Or those school days with Baby Phat jeans,
    And lip gloss so shiny
    You swore you could see your reflection in it.

Hustlin' in the hallways,
trading notes with your girls,
Talkin' about who liked who,
Crushing on that boy you'd never talk to,
    But wrote his name in your notebook a hundred times.

The smell of pink lotion,
    That one brown couch every grandma had,
    And front porch sittin' like it was a throne.
    We didn't have much,
    But what we had was rich—

Rich in laughter, rich in culture,
Rich in love that never needed explaining.

We grew up with the kind of soul
    You can't bottle, can't buy.
That old-school life?
    That's what raised us.

The rhythms, the rituals, the realness.
    And even now,
    when the world tries to move too fast,
    I hold onto it,
    That nostalgia wrapped in the smell of Mama's kitchen,
    In the sound of her voice singing me awake.
That's home.

EVERYBODY'S FAVORITE AUNTIE

Auntie?

She ain't just your second mama—
she's the vibe you wish Mama had time for.
Let you sneak a little more freedom,
sips of life Mama wouldn't dare pour.
She's the loud laugh at every cookout,
the one who knows how to turn up the fun,
but best believe she'll check you quick
because Auntie don't play when it's all said and done.

> She got stories that Mama won't spill—
> about how wild she used to be,
> about that boy who thought he could break her,
> and the one who swept her off her feet, finally free.
> Auntie will pull you to the side with a wink,
> "Girl, don't let nobody dim that light,"
> or, "You bet not be messin' with him,
> I see that fool comin' a mile in plain sight."

Her house?
It's the escape, the hideaway, the haven—
when Mama's on your back, and you just need some saving.
Fridge? Always stocked.
Hugs? Always on lock.
And her advice? Baby, it's got spice—
the kind Mama don't serve, but you crave in life.
"You better know you fine just as you are,
and don't you dare shrink for no man or star!"

> Auntie been through it; she sees it in your eyes,
> knows the storm brewing before you even realize.

Beneath Her Cracked Armor She Blooms

She'll read your vibe, feel what you need,
and when the world's heavy? She gives you that space to breathe.
Borrow her clothes, raid her closet,
try on her heels like you running the world—
Auntie's been there, done that,
and baby, she'll tell you how not to crash and burn.

She pulls you aside with that seasoned talk,
teaches you how to hustle, how to walk that boss walk.
"You better strut, baby, even in a storm,
this world will try you—stand tall, reform."
And just when you think you're grown enough to test her?
One look, and she'll have you in check—
that Auntie-stare cold enough to freeze your breath.
"You better know your worth, sugar,
'cause this world will have you forgettin' you a treasure."

She ain't playing about love, about life,
about making sure you ain't settling for strife.
Auntie is the one who taught you to hold your head high,
to love deep, but walk away when it ain't right.
How to laugh through the tears,
and always, always come back harder,
like the woman she is,
like the woman you're becoming—
stronger.

Auntie's love?
It's that warmth wrapped in cool,
the extra seasoning in life's stew.
You don't know you need it 'til she ain't around,
and suddenly, you're missing that sound—
that cackle, that side-eye, that real.
She made sure you never walked this life alone,
'cause Auntie always got your back, no matter what.

Beneath Her Cracked Armor She Blooms

She's like Mama, but with more soul,
more flavor, more stories to make you whole.

Auntie showed you how to laugh even when it hurts,
how to love fiercely, but still know your worth.
She'll ride for you 'til the wheels fall off,
got the wisdom of a sage, the sass of a boss.
Auntie's that secret sauce,
the glue you didn't even know you needed—
until she's not there, and you feel it,
like a missing piece of yourself.

> **So, here's to Auntie, the one who showed you**
> **how to be free,**
> **how to rise, how to shine,**
> **how to keep your flavor strong,**
> **no matter the grind.**

Beneath Her Cracked Armor She Blooms

THE ENGINE THAT KEEPS RUNNING"

She's built tough,
like the best kind of car that never breaks down,
the kind that's been running for years,
through miles of trials,
and still gets you where you need to go.
Her body's the chassis,
her heart's the engine,
and she moves like a machine—steady, smooth,
even when the road is full of potholes.

She was made for endurance,
like an old-school Cadillac or a souped-up Chevy,
engine purring under the hood,
ready to take on whatever comes next.
She's been through the winters,
the snowstorms of life,
but her tires?
They still grip the road.
She doesn't slip.

Every morning,
she's up before the sun—
like clockwork, reliable.
Oil's checked, tank's full,
she's out here running errands,
hustling, grinding,
getting her people where they need to be.
She's the ride everyone depends on,
because they know—
no matter what,
she'll get them there.

Her heart hums like an engine
built to last,
with a rhythm that never skips a beat.
She's got the kind of horsepower

Beneath Her Cracked Armor She Blooms

you only read about,
and she keeps moving,
keeps running,
even when the miles start adding up.
No breakdowns,
just tune-ups—
because she knows how to keep herself going,
even when the world tries to wear her down.

And let's not forget the bodywork—
smooth, sleek, always polished.
She shines,
even when the road's been rough.
Her paint might chip,
her tires might squeal,
but she'll never let you see her stop.
She's classic, timeless,
and even if she gets a little scratched up,
her worth doesn't drop.

You see, she's been built for this—
a machine finely tuned,
born to run on high octane
and push through the days
when the load gets too heavy.
She's carried it all—
the groceries, the kids, the dreams she never let go of.
And she's still rolling.

Her gas light?
Yeah, it's been on,
but she still makes it to the finish line,
because a Black woman knows
how to keep going,
how to coast when the tank's running low,
how to refuel herself
with nothing but faith and grit.

She doesn't get parked,
doesn't sit idle—
always in drive,

Beneath Her Cracked Armor She Blooms

always ready to hit the next road.
And even when she pulls into the garage at night,
she's planning the next day's route,
because rest is just a pit stop
for a woman who's got places to be.

So here's to her—
the good working car that never quits,
the Black woman whose engine never dies,
whose drive is unstoppable.
She's a force on four wheels,
a machine that refuses to rust,
because she knows that no matter the terrain,
she was built to last.

STRESS BE KILLING US, SIS

You ever feel that chokehold—
The weight that grips tight like you're always on hold,
Like your breath just can't catch a break?
They call it *stress,* but let's be clear—
It's not just tension in the shoulders,
It's the silent thief in the night,
A slow bleed we've normalized
While the world tells us to just "keep fighting."

But this fight?
It's claiming lives.
We're soldiers in a war we never signed up for,
And baby, it's killing us quicker than we know.
Black women?
We're dying young—
Not from bullets, but from the stress of simply *being*.
Carrying the weight of expectations
With no room for ease.

Facts don't play:
Heart disease is the number one slayer
Of sisters like you and me.
Hypertension creeps like a snake in the grass,
Sinks its fangs into our veins,
Blood pressure rising like the rage we bottle up—
They wonder why we scream, why we snap.
Sis, it's because stress is carving up our insides,

Leaving scars they can't see,
But we *feel*.

Data speaks louder than we ever could:
We're 60% more likely to be walking with that pressure,
Pressure that comes not from choice but from survival.
Twice as likely to drop from strokes
While trying to keep the peace,
But who's keeping *us*?
The body bears the burden—
Every bill unpaid, every word unsaid,
The trauma we inherit and the care we never get.

You know what stress does?
It don't just knock on the door,
It barges in, sets up shop,
Uninvited but expected.
It takes up space in our bones,
Turns heartbeats into ticking time bombs.
They say, "Strong Black woman,"
But that strength has a price,
And the cost is our lives.
We've been bending for too long,
Until the breaking feels like breathing.

Stress is a shadow we've learned to live in,
But it don't play fair.
It whispers lies—
"You can take it. Keep going. You don't need rest."
But every heartbeat says different.
That pulse you feel?
It's the drumline of generations,
And sis, it's been pounding too hard for too long.

Beneath Her Cracked Armor She Blooms

Our mothers, our grandmothers—
They carried the weight,
But nobody told us it's okay to set it down.
This stress?
It's been passed down like an heirloom,
Wrapped in survival and sacrifice,
But baby, we can't wear it forever.

The science says it all:
When the cortisol stays too high,
It turns your body into a battleground.
Heart disease, strokes—
They're not accidents; they're the outcome
Of a life lived under siege.
And Black women?
We're twice as likely to fall.
Because stress don't discriminate,
But the system does,
And we're left trying to catch up,
Chasing a breath we never seem to find.

So, what's the solution?
It's not in pushing harder,
But in reclaiming ease.
It's in knowing that rest is a right,
Not a reward for survival.
It's in breaking the silence that says we have to hold it all,
Because if we don't speak,
We die with our mouths closed
And our hearts heavy.

So, sis—
Breathe.
Let that exhale carry the weight of the generations before you,

Beneath Her Cracked Armor She Blooms

Let it remind you that your softness is sacred,
That you are worthy of peace,
Of lightness,
Of letting go.
This stress?
It's not yours to bear alone.
And no, we ain't strong because we *have* to be—
We're strong because we choose to be,
But it's time we choose *life*.

HANDS THAT HEAL

These hands,
they've been through the fire,
held heat in silence,
worked under pressure,
but never retired.
They've carried burdens that weren't mine to bear,
turned pain into productivity,
like alchemy in the air.

I used to think healing was something soft,
something delicate,
but hell no—
they are lying,
it's brutal.
Healing what you make it.
It's the work you do when no one's watching,
the digging you do when no one is listening.
Healing is sweat and stillness.
It's learning to take these same hands.
that have been stretched thin.
and teach them to rest,
to hold,
to mend.

These hands?
They've cradled dreams that felt too big,
too heavy for this frame.

But they held on anyway,
because letting go was never an option.
They've built bridges from brokenness,
stitched up souls that bled from years of neglect,
including my own.

They know the language of labor,
but they're learning the art of care.
See, healing isn't always about fixing,
sometimes it's about feeling—
it's about laying your hands on your own wounds.
and saying, "It's okay to be hurt,
it's okay to need repair."

And yes, these hands get tired.
They ache from giving,
from holding too much for too long.
But I'm learning to put them down,
to let them rest,
Not everything needs to be built.
Not everything needs to be held up.

Sometimes healing is found in the letting go,
in the release,
in the way your fingers finally open
after years of holding on too tight.

But make no mistake—
these hands have power.
Not because they are perfect,
but because they know how to rise,
even after they've been burned.

Beneath Her Cracked Armor She Blooms

They know how to create,
how to love,
how to heal
without asking for permission.
They are my first responders,
in a world that takes without asking,
and now, they take back.

Hands that once only knew how to give
are learning to receive.
Hands that carried the world
                        ARE LEARNING TO CARRY ME.

RELAX, REST, AND RESET

She wakes up, and for the first time in a long while,
the world can wait.
Today, she can do what she likes to do,
and go at her own pace.
Today she will not enter the race
because it's alright, beautiful, to just take time for you.

This morning, there's no alarm clock rushing her through,
no hands pulling her, no names calling too.
No kids begging for bites of her plate,
no deadlines, no chores, no plans running late.

Today is all hers.
She slips into softness,
not the kind she shows for others,
but the kind that holds her—
a robe that whispers "breathe,"
a cup of tea that steams like release.

Just her, sinking into the quiet,
letting go of the weight she's carried for everyone else.

Today, she's not a mother, not a sister,
not a friend or worker, no duties to list her.
She's just her.
And in this space, she stretches,
reaches into the parts of herself
that have been waiting for her touch.

Beneath Her Cracked Armor She Blooms

She lets her body rest,
her mind rest,
her heart take a break.
The world will be there tomorrow—
but today?
She will light some candles and blast some Anita Baker,
because she is giving the best that she got to her.

And....

She sure does deserve it,
though she'd never admit it.
She's been everything to everyone but herself,
and now she knows she'll burn out that way—
that isn't okay.

So, in this moment she will,
relax, rest, recoup, reset.
Read a book, chill,
maybe roll up and vibe out,
whatever she feels.

And when the sun sets on this day,
she'll rise tomorrow with new breath,
new strength,
ready to give again.

SACRED GROUND

Her home ain't just four walls—
it's where her spirit calls.
A sacred space, where the world can't chase,
and she can finally rest her all.

The kitchen hums with soul food sounds,
spices passed down, all around.
Grandmama's prayers simmer on the stove,
where strength is cooked, and love is bold.

In the living room, she finds her peace,
feet moving slow, the world's release.
Candles flicker, the light never fades,
where ancestors' songs softly play.

Her bedroom's where dreams take flight,
under warm covers, she's safe at night.
The world outside can't reach her here,
this is where she sheds the fear.

Outside, she's strong, but here she's free,
a queen at home in her majesty.
It's more than a house—this is her space,
her sacred ground, her resting place.

Beneath Her Cracked Armor She Blooms

GET UP QUEEN

So, Get Up Queen,
Far too long have you been asleep.
Rise to cause havoc and to bring these people some peace.
As the sun rises and the moon sets,
Your power isn't in waiting—it's in motion,
A storm brewing in silence, ready to be unleashed.
In all your fears, just let go, Queen.

This world wasn't built for you to shrink—
It was built to witness your stretch,
your reach, your rise,
unapologetic and bold.
As your clock resets, remember,
your purpose is in your dreams,
in the whispers of your ancestors,
the ones who carved their wisdom into your bones.
You are not here to just survive—
you are here to thrive,
to turn the soil beneath your feet into gold.

Let your third eye guide.
Breathe in the universe that lives within you.
Focus. Love. Forgive. Heal.
You are more than what the world told you to be—
you are what it fears you will become.
In thy own majestic greatness, believe.

Rise, Queen, in all your regal power.
Shake the earth with your presence,
let them feel the rumble of your heart beating
with every step.

Beneath Her Cracked Armor She Blooms

You were never meant to be small,
never meant to tiptoe through life unnoticed.
You were born to disrupt the stillness,
to break the silence with your voice
and rewrite the rules with your grace.

Your crown was never lost; it was simply waiting
for you to remember where you placed it.
Lift your head, wear it high,
for in your resilience,
the universe finds its balance.
Know that even when you stumble,
you are still royal in every fall,
because the ground beneath you bows
in the presence of your rise.

Breathe,
not because they expect you to,
but because the breath you hold is sacred.
It is the echo of every woman before you
who dared to exhale in a world that sought to silence her.
You are the continuation of that breath,
the embodiment of resilience wrapped in softness. So, Get up,
Queen,

Far too long have you been asleep.
Rise to cause havoc and to bring these people some peace.
As the sun rises and the moon sets
In all your fears, just let go, queen,

As your clock resets remember your purpose is in your dreams.
Let's your third eye guide. Breath.
Focus. Love. Forgive. Heal!
In thy own majestic greatness believe.

LEMONADE & HEALING

*We learned the art of making do,
turning sour into something sweet.
Mama taught us early on
how to flip pain on its feet.*

*We press light from dark days,
squeeze hope from the toughest places.
Turn struggle into sustenance,
pour healing into broken spaces.*

*This isn't new—
it's how we rise,
not despite the weight,
but because we carry it inside.*

*We take what was meant to break us,
and make it whole.
Pour it out like lemonade,*

UNCHAIN ME

I used to think staying small
was where I should be,
shrinking,
hiding—
because that's all I could see.
I let doubt settle deep,
hoping that if I held on long enough,
the fear would fade,
and the weight would lift off of me.

But now I know—
it wasn't me who was stuck,
it's fear that held me back,
with its relentless grip,
a shadow I didn't ask to hold.

I played it safe,
in the corners of who I thought I had to be,
thinking staying unseen
was safer
than stepping out free.

But love—
real love—
was never supposed to feel like chains.

Beneath Her Cracked Armor She Blooms

It wasn't made to keep me still,
or hold me down,
or make me question
if I'm worthy of the crown.
It's not meant to circle
the same doubts
that kept me grounded.

I thought staying in this comfort
was strength—
but real strength?
It's in letting go.

So today,
I choose me.
I choose the voice
I silenced
so I could keep my fears close.
I choose joy—
the kind that grows inside,
without anyone's permission.

I choose freedom,
because love should set me free,
not bind me to a version
that no longer fits me.

I used to think I needed this,
that I couldn't be whole
without playing it safe.
But now I know—
I've always been whole,
I just didn't claim it.

Beneath Her Cracked Armor She Blooms

You don't get to hold me back,
or keep me safe in the shadows
while I shrink.
I'm picking up the pieces
that I left behind,
and as I rise,
I rise with fire—
head held high,
unchained from the weight of before.

Love should lift,
not drag me down.
It should stoke the fire,
not dim the flame.

I refuse to stay hidden,
to keep shrinking,
to stay in the past
I've long outgrown.
I deserve more than this

UNAPOLOGIZING

                                        I'm done explaining myself.
Done
        tiptoeing
            around
                feelings,
watering myself down so they can swallow me easier.
I'm done saying I'm sorry when I don't mean it,
just to make somebody else feel better about their shit.

I ain't apologizing for my hustle,
for working harder than most,
for getting up when they swore, I'd stay down.
I'm done apologizing for the grind,
for wanting more, for going after what's mine.
I don't owe you shit.
I ain't sorry for my mouth,
for the way I speak my truth, loud and clear.

You can call it an attitude,
but I call it knowing my worth.
I've earned this fire—
And you're just mad you can't put it out.

I'm done apologizing for choosing me.
Yes, I said no.

I'm allowed to pick myself for once,
to put my peace before your drama,
to step back from all your problems
and protect me.
And guess what?
I'm not sorry for it.

I'm done explaining why I'm still single,
why I haven't settled down yet,
why my kids are being raised my way, not yours.
I'm not sorry for my ambition.
For wanting more than the scraps they hand out.
For making moves they said weren't for me.
I ain't apologizing for my anger,
for the way it simmers beneath the surface
when I've simply have had enough.
If you don't like the way I speak my truth,
then hey, that's totally on you

I'm done explaining why I walk how I walk,
talk how I talk,
why I move how I move.
If I tell the truth, I've spent too many years apologizing too,
for things that ain't my fault.
Being sorry for the lesson you weren't taught.

But this life, it's mine.
I'm gonna live it loud,
I'm gonna live it proud,
and if you don't like it,
that's your problem, not mine.
I would say my bad but
I ain't apologizing for shit!

STEPS TO NOT GIVING A F*CK

Step 1: Don't pick up the guilt they're trying to hand you.
They'll show up with expectations tied in bows,
But you ain't obligated to play that role.
Not today, not tomorrow.
Your peace? It's yours to borrow.
If they call, let it ring.
If they text, let it sit.
You owe nobody your time,
And trust—you're just fine with it.

Step 2: Keep your money your business.
"Why spend that much on yourself?" they'll ask.
But it ain't their business, don't even unmask.
Why not?
Their judgment won't pay your bills.
Whether it's a trip or fresh new heels,
They can sit on the sidelines of your spree.
This bag? It's yours, sis—go get it, guilt-free.

Step 3: Stop justifying your boundaries.
Set them high, lock them tight—no need to explain.
Let them knock on doors where they won't remain.
If they weren't invited, don't hand 'em a key.
Your peace is sacred, guard it carefully.

Ain't no need to apologize, not even a chance,
You control your energy, and this ain't a dance.

Step 4: Don't let social media set your standards.
Their likes don't define your worth or glow,
Their comments don't control your flow.
You live this life, not for their eyes—
You're out here winning, don't need their "highs."
Your victories don't need a public stage,
Keep thriving, keep flipping the page.

Step 5: Family isn't a free pass to your energy.
Just because they share your blood,
Doesn't mean they get to drain the flood.
"No" is a sentence, complete and real,
A boundary they better learn to feel.
If they ask, "Why you so distant?"
Shrug and sip your peace, it's consistent.

Step 6: Love yourself without conditions.
You don't need no man to make it right,
Don't need a partner to hold you tight.
This journey? Sis, it's all your own,
Learn what makes you smile—alone.
Take yourself out, set the tone,
No guilt for making yourself feel at home.

Step 7: Let people handle their own mess.
Stop being their emotional rest,
Let them deal with their own stress.
You're not the blanket for their rain,
Your job is to protect your peace,

To maintain.
Their drama? Sis, that is not your load,
Don't let them pull you down that road.

Step 8: Celebrate your small wins like they're big ones.
Cooked a meal? Took a nap? Made it through?
That's a win, and sis, it's for you.
Don't wait for some award or check,
Clap for yourself, stand tall and flex.
You're living, breathing, doing your best,
Celebrate yourself—now, rest.

Step 9: Speak your truth without a filter.
Too bold, too raw, too loud?
They can hush, while you stay proud.
You weren't made to fit their mold,
Your truth's a treasure, and its gold.
Say what's on your mind, be you,
Let 'em deal with the discomfort too.

Step 10: Walk away when it's time.
Don't stick around when it drains your shine.
Whether it's a job, a friend, or a draining place,
Cut it off without a trace.
You deserve peace, not obligation.
Walk away, no hesitation.

GOD GAVE YOU DOMINION OVER THE EARTH

Get your passport,
because this world was never meant to keep you small.
They built walls around you—called them borders,
told you, *stay here, don't crawl,*
but Sis, let me remind you—
you belong to it all.
The soil under your feet doesn't care for boundaries,
and the sky doesn't fall in one language.
It's time to break free of that box they placed you in,
where your roots dug deep,
but never got to stretch thin.

They brought our ancestors across oceans,
packed tight in the belly of ships.
But those waters?
We command them now—
what once carried chains now carries our ships and planes.
We fly over the same seas that sought to erase us,
writing new stories in places that once displaced us.

Go wake up in Ghana,
watch the sun paint the sky a shade
you've only ever dreamed in.
Let it kiss your skin with a warmth
that knows your name without asking.
Walk the streets and listen—
not to the poverty they show you,

Beneath Her Cracked Armor She Blooms

but to the hum,
to the stories of life, bold and bright,
in every step, every breath, every laugh.

Africa isn't the image they sold.
It's not weak, not broken—
it's gold.
Its resilience wrapped in beauty,
waiting for you to unfold.
The land calls you home,
it's not a foreign space.
Every face you pass feels familiar,
and every street you walk holds your grace.

Step outside the city,
outside the lines they drew for you.
This world is yours to move through.
Stamp that passport,
not just with names, but with your legacy,
because you're not just a descendant—
you are the seed that survived.
The one they didn't plan to see thrive.

They'll tell you travel's a luxury,
something you can't afford.
But they don't know your story.
You're the one who wakes on mountaintops,
the one who feels freedom in the same air
they thought would break you.
Take a selfie with the clouds,
write your name in sand that sings with your history.
Let the Nile teach you its rhythm,
let Morocco show you how the stars align
to trace your name through time.

Beneath Her Cracked Armor She Blooms

Eat food that tastes like ancestors,
flavors that speak of survival and victory.
You are a global traveler,
rooted in the past but reaching forward—
no longer tethered to what was.

Sis, God gave you the earth to claim.
Walk it.
It's yours to love, to see, to touch,
to breathe in every corner,
to stand where your ancestors once dreamed,
and to live in the places they couldn't reach.

This planet is yours,
one flight, one sunrise, one step at a time.
Take it back.
The world is waiting—

so **go**!

Beneath Her Cracked Armor She Blooms

CROOKLYN

I've never been to Brooklyn,
Never sat on a brownstone stoop,
But *Crooklyn* felt like home,
Like I lived there too.
A Black girl from nowhere near those streets,
But Troy?
She could've been me,
Or any of us.

I watched that screen like it was my own window,
Peeking into a world that felt familiar,
Even though I never ran down those blocks,
Never hollered at neighbors or heard Mama call me in from play.
But something about that house,
About that family,
Hit close.
Maybe it was the way they laughed through the mess,
Or how they loved even when they fought.
Maybe it was the way the music carried through the air,
Like a soundtrack to Black survival.

Troy was all of us,
Learning to be strong before she knew what strength meant.
Navigating the push and pull of love in a family that wasn't perfect,
But was real.
She wore those braids like a crown,
Held her own in the middle of the noise,
And I felt that.
Even from miles away,
I knew what it was to carry the weight,
To be young but still feel grown,
To laugh when you wanted to cry.

I never smelled the street vendors,
Never heard the sound of dominoes slapping the table outside,

Beneath Her Cracked Armor She Blooms

But *Crooklyn* made me feel like I had.
Like I knew that world,
Even though my block didn't look the same.
The family gatherings, the cousins running wild,
The old heads with their stories—
It all felt like I'd lived it,
Like Troy's life and mine weren't so far apart.

I saw myself in her,
In the way she loved her family,
Even when things fell apart.
I felt her heartbreak,
Felt her strength,
Felt her learning to stand tall
In a world that doesn't always let Black girls be soft.
And even though I wasn't there,
Wasn't on that stoop,
I was with her.

Crooklyn wasn't just a movie—
It was a memory I didn't know I had.
A reminder that no matter where we're from,
Black girlhood carries a rhythm of its own.
A rhythm that doesn't need Brooklyn's streets to be understood,
A rhythm that beats in the kitchens, in the living rooms,
In every place we call home.
And maybe I've never been to Crooklyn,
But somehow,
It's been with me all along

Beneath Her Cracked Armor She Blooms

STANDING ALONE

There's a moment when you realize—
nobody's coming to save you.
Sounds harsh, right?
But, girl, there's power in that view.
That's when you stop waiting,
stop explaining,
stop caring who's watching or who's hating.
It's not loneliness, it's liberation.
When you stand alone, you're standing tall,
with every piece of yourself—unbreakable, whole.
No one to mold you, no one to dilute,
no one to bend you to fit their pursuit.

Yeah, they'll talk,
they'll say, "Too independent."
As if that's a flaw, not a compliment.
Like you were made to be anything less
than a force, than a truth they can't suppress.
You ever notice how "alone" makes them squirm?
Like your worth depends on someone confirming.
But, your worth runs deep,
rooted in the soil that refuses to sleep.

We've stood alone since they told us we had to be
both strong and soft,
both provider and shield.
We've been the warrior and the calm,
nurtured others while dropping bombs of truth.

Beneath Her Cracked Armor She Blooms

And still, we rise,
on our own time, with no disguise.

Standing alone doesn't mean you're cold.
It means you're free,
free from their hold.
Free from their expectations,
their need for control,
free from their judgments on how you roll.
They want you to fold, fit in their box,
but you're too wide, too vast—unorthodox.
You're your own woman, unchained, untamed.
And when you stand alone, you ain't empty.
You're rooted in history,
with every Black woman who's ever been told
she's too much, or not enough, too bold.

Standing alone is a rebellion,
a protest to their cage,
saying, "I don't need your approval
to breathe, to thrive, or to rage."
We've been doing this since forever,
standing at the crossroad of love and pain,
of hope and heartbreak,
rising again and again.

Let them call it what they want—
independent, unattached, single, "strong."
You call it freedom,
choosing yourself over their song.
And when the dust settles,
when the noise dies down,
you'll still be standing,
wearing your crown.
Alone? Nah,
you're standing with every woman
who's ever broken free.

Beneath Her Cracked Armor She Blooms

THE ART OF PETTY

See, petty ain't childish—
it's a calculated move,
A chess game where I don't even have to move.
It's the silence that speaks louder than words,
the look that says "I peeped it"
but I ain't shook, I ain't disturbed.

You think I forgot?
Like the generations before me? Nah.
We keep receipts like legacies.
I learned from the best—my aunties, my mama, my gran—
how to master the art of the upper hand.
Petty runs deep, it's in the bloodline,
a quiet clapback, a subtle rewind.

It's the phone call I won't return,
the bridge you thought you'd burn—
but I rebuilt it, crossed it,
and left you to learn.
Petty ain't about anger, nah, it's restraint,
Cause I could ruin your world,
but I won't—it ain't worth the paint.

You ever see a Black woman sit still,
eyes low, while you spill?
That's not ignorance, love,

Beneath Her Cracked Armor She Blooms

That's me letting you think you won,
while I move with a different kind of grace,
mapping out my next step without showing my face.

It's in the "Oh, I'm fine,"
when you know I ain't.
But best believe when you stumble,
I won't even blink.
I'm too grown for the mess,
but don't get it confused—
I can play this game better than you ever could choose.

Petty's like art—it's in the small things,
Not always loud, but it still stings.
It's remembering every slight you thought I'd forget,
and using it like currency with no regret.
It's not in the loud cuss-outs or the fights,
it's in the way I live rent-free in your mind at night.

I'll send you flowers for the win you bragged about,
knowing full well my silence speaks louder than your shout.
I don't need to get loud to prove my worth,
I just let karma do its slow burn, watch the earth.

It's knowing you can't touch what's already blessed,
so I'll smile, sip tea,
and let you stress.
You'll see me glowing while you're still guessing,
'cause the best part of petty?
Is never confessing.

So no, I don't have to raise my voice,
I just play the cards I know will make you lose choice.

Beneath Her Cracked Armor She Blooms

I learned from Black women who've seen it all before—
who stood tall while the world tried to settle the score.

Petty's an art,
and I've mastered it well,
a quiet power,
a story I won't tell.
You keep playing, thinking you've won,
But baby, I ain't even started—I'm just having fun.

I'M FINE"

"How you doing?" they ask,
and I throw out the easiest lie I know—
"I'm fine."
Because fine is what they wanna hear,
it's what keeps the conversation moving.
Fine is the mask I've been wearing so long,
I forget what I look like without it.
But underneath, it's a different story.

Black women, we're taught to wear strength
like a second skin,
to smile through the struggle,
to laugh while we carry the weight of the world.
But who's holding us up
when we're falling apart inside?

We learned to say "I'm fine"
when what we really mean is:
"I'm tired."
I'm tired of smiling through the pain,
tired of acting like I've got it all together,
like I'm not breaking down
piece by piece.

You ask me how I'm doing,
but do you really wanna know?
Do you wanna hear about the sleepless nights,
the anxiety that creeps up on me like a shadow,
the depression I fight off with every breath?

Nah, you just want "fine."
And I get it,
because fine keeps it simple,
keeps it neat.
But fine don't fix what's broken.

Beneath Her Cracked Armor She Blooms

I've been masking so long,
I've got cracks under the makeup,
but you won't see those.
You'll just see the smile,
the way I laugh it off
like everything's cool.

But Black women know—
we know what it's like to hold it down,
to hold it in,
to hold it together
when nobody's checking for us.
They call it strength,
but really, it's survival.

I've been called strong my whole life,
but strong don't mean unbreakable.
Strong means tired.
Strong means carrying everyone else's weight
and barely holding onto your own.

And therapy?
Yeah, I'm in it,
but sometimes it feels like a Band-Aid on a wound too deep to close.
How do you explain trauma that's been passed down,
like hand-me-down clothes you never wanted to wear?

They don't talk about mental illness in our homes—
we sweep it under the rug,
smile for the cameras,
and keep it moving.
But that silence is heavy,
and I've been carrying it too long.

So no, I'm not fine.
I'm not okay.
I'm holding on,
barely.
I've been burning at both ends,
and I'm tired of pretending the fire doesn't hurt.

Beneath Her Cracked Armor She Blooms

But here's the truth—
I deserve to say "I'm not fine"
without the world looking away,
without feeling like I'm failing just because I'm human.
We deserve more than "strong."
We deserve space to rest,
to heal,
to be seen beyond the mask.

So next time you ask me how I'm doing,
don't expect the same old lie.
Because I'm done with pretending.
I'm done with "fine."

MONSTERS

It started with a story—
    the kind you tell kids when the night feels too quiet,
    when the wind brushes the windows like a whisper
    and the shadows stretch longer than they should.
I used to believe monsters lived under the bed,
    small enough to hide in the dark corners
but big enough to make me keep my feet tucked tight under the covers.

I thought I outgrew that fear.
You know, the one that makes you check the closet
before turning out the light,
makes you double-check the lock on the door
before you close your eyes.

But now, I realize the monsters never left.
They just found new homes.
No longer content to sit under my bed—
they've
    crawled
        into my head,
set up shop in the spaces where dreams used to live.
Now they turn my sleep into a battlefield,
and the nightmares don't end when I wake up.

I'm walking through dreams like a maze,
dodging monsters that wear faces I recognize,
that whisper my fears like they've memorized my secrets.

I run, but the ground pulls me back—
my legs don't move as fast as my mind.
I scream, but the sound gets swallowed
by the silence of my own doubt.

These nightmares are no longer made of shadows.
        They're made of real things:
            the unpaid bills stacked on the counter,
           the deadlines that chase me into the night,
   the faces of people who left but never really disappeared.
       They haunt me,
not with claws and teeth,
but with
words left unsaid,
with
guilt,
regret,
and the weight of not being enough.

The monsters aren't under my bed.
They are in the missed opportunities,
the dreams deferred,
the moments I let slip away.

I wake up, heart ***pounding,***
but the nightmare doesn't fade.
It follows me into the day............................
a living, breathing thing that takes my hand
and walks with me like a shadow.
I can't shake it off.
==It clings to my thoughts,==
turns every step into a stumble,
every breath into a question.

Beneath Her Cracked Armor She Blooms

There's no waking up from this,
no safety of daylight to run to.
These monsters have faces,
they pay rent in my mind,
they're woven into the fabric of every sleepless night.
There is no escape, only confrontation.
So, I face them.

No saviors here.
Just me and the monsters.
And tonight, I'm not the one who's running.

CHECK ON YOUR STRONG FRIEND

She's the one they all turn to—
solid, unshaken, like she don't bend.
But even the strongest oak sways in the wind,
even the deepest well runs dry,
and sometimes, she needs a hand
but won't ever ask why.

Check on her, the one who holds it down
like the weight of the world is hers to carry.
She's your strong friend,
but strength doesn't mean she's never weary.
She's learned to smile through it,
learned to lift while falling apart—
but when was the last time you asked her
what's really in her heart?

They say, "Strong Black woman,"
like it's a badge of pride,
but they don't see the cracks,
the moments she's cried
behind closed doors,
because strong don't mean bulletproof,
and nobody notices
when she's standing on the edge of truth.

She's the first to show up,
the last to complain,
but her shoulders are heavy
from carrying everybody else's pain.
They see her shine,
but they don't ask if it's dimming inside.
They don't see the nights she's barely surviving,
the days she's questioning her own mind.

Check on her—
not because she'll ask,

Beneath Her Cracked Armor She Blooms

but because she won't.
Not because she looks tired,
but because she's been carrying more
than anyone knows.

She's strong,
but she's also human.
And sometimes, even steel gets tired of holding the weight.
Even the sun needs a break from the sky.
Her strength is in her survival,
but survival ain't the goal—
it's peace, it's rest,
it's finally feeling whole.

Do you know the statistics?
Black women are more likely to shoulder the mental load,
less likely to get the care they need,
because strength is what they've been sold.
It's the invisible labor,
the silent tears,
the "I'm fine" that covers years of fear.
Anxiety's rising, depression's real,
but she don't get to slow down—
that's the deal.

Check on her—
because while she's lifting everyone else,
nobody's lifting her.
She's more than the strong one,
she's more than just a shield.
She deserves a space to fall,
a place where her wounds can heal.

Strong doesn't mean she's unbreakable,
it just means she's been holding on
to pieces that need space to breathe.
So check on your strong friend,
the one you think never needs you—
because sometimes,
she's the one who needs it most

BEATING THE FACE TO COVER THE BEATING

She's standing in the mirror,
hands trembling like yesterday's tears,
foundation brush in hand—
they call it "beating the face,"
but today it's covering the bruises,
masking the places where his fists hit hardest.

How ironic, she's calling out to God
while beating her face to the Gods,
like the girlies say—
as if this palette can paint over the pain,
as if primer can smooth the bruises
he left in her spirit.
It's ritual now.
The routine of hiding the aftermath,
the strokes of concealer over the purples and blues,
layering on the lies thick,
thicker than the words she doesn't dare speak.

This ain't just makeup,
this is being strong in a bottle.
She starts with the primer,
not for her skin but for her soul,
as if smoothing it over can make her feel whole again.
As if blending it in could erase
the memories of last night,
when he called her out her name,
when her body folded under his anger.
But she blends anyway,
because who's got time to fall apart?
Foundation comes next,

Beneath Her Cracked Armor She Blooms

the paradox of building something solid
on top of something so broken.

She picks her shade—
just the right brown to cover the bruises,
the ones that bloom under her eyes
and across her jawline.
She pats it in, soft at first,
then harder—
a beat that mimics the rhythm
of fists against her skin.
She reaches for the concealer—
this is where the real work begins.
This is the eraser,
the tool that makes it all disappear,
or at least, that's what she tells herself.

Under the eyes first,
to cover the nights she didn't sleep,
the nights she stayed awake praying
that this time would be different,
that this time the man she loved
wouldn't turn into a monster
.
She dabs it over her cheek,
over the place where his hand landed hardest.
It's not about looking perfect—
it's about looking okay,
like nothing's wrong,
like her life ain't a war zone.
Contour, highlight—
she carves out the features
she used to love about herself.
She sculpts her cheeks,
sharp enough to cut through the silence,
to give herself the strength
to face the world outside.

Beneath Her Cracked Armor She Blooms

Her nose?
Slim it down, make it sleek,
so, no one sees the way it flares
when she holds back tears.
Eyeshadow next—
but it's not about glamor.
It's about distraction.
She smokes it out,
makes it dramatic,
so no one sees the cracks in her soul.
Winged liner, sharp and bold,
because if her eyes are fierce enough,
maybe they won't notice the fear
that lives behind them.

She adds the blush—
rosy on the cheeks,
covering the red he left behind.
She paints on a smile
where there's only been sorrow,
brushes on the warmth
that life has stolen from her.

Last, the lips—
red, because red is loud,
red says "Look at me,"
when all she really wants
is to disappear.
She lines them perfect,
paints them thick,
hides the words she never speaks
behind the color.
And then, the setting spray.
She holds it in the air like a shield,
a final layer of protection,
because once it's locked in,

Beneath Her Cracked Armor She Blooms

she can't crack.
She can't let anyone see
the girl behind the face.
This mask must last—
through the stares, through the whispers,
through the questions she ain't ready to answer.

How ironic,
that she's calling out to God
while beating her face to the God—
hoping this face can hold her together,
hide the bruises both seen and unseen.
She looks in the mirror one last time,
and for a second,
she almost believes the illusion.
Almost

HEAVINESS CARRIES THE HEART

Grief is not a shadow—
it is the weight in the bones,
a heaviness so familiar, it shapes you
before you can name it.
I never invited grief inside,
but somehow, it found the cracks in my smile,
settling into the spaces where joy used to live.

They say time is a healer,
but what does time know of this kind of silence?
Of how the heart beats slower when burdened?
How the mind loops through memories
like trying to solve a puzzle with missing pieces.
I have learned that time does not soothe—it only suspends.
Grief, like gravity, never really let's go.

There are days when I wake up forgetting,
only to remember in the quiet moments
that there is something I'm carrying
that cannot be put down.
Heavy is the heart that loves and loses,
but heavier still is the soul that survives
despite the weight.

I speak to grief like an old friend,

Beneath Her Cracked Armor She Blooms

knowing it's not a battle to be won
but a language to be learned.
It has no answers, just echoes.
I've asked it for peace,
and it responds with more questions.

How do you rebuild a foundation
that was never steady?
How do you heal a wound that never closes?
I've stitched myself together with silence,
knowing that some things will always bleed
just beneath the skin.

But even in the bleeding, there is grace.
The kind that is quiet, unspoken,
a strength that has nothing to prove.
I don't rise every day to be a symbol,
I rise because my body knows no other way.
Because living is not always about triumph—
sometimes it's about endurance.

Heavy is the heart, yes—
but there's something sacred in the weight.
A knowing that in the breaking,
there is wisdom.
In the holding on, there is power.
And in the grief,
there is a love so deep, it cannot be forgotten.

MY SISTER GOT ME

My sister, she got this way of knowing me better than I know myself, like a mirror that don't crack even when my reflection feels too heavy to hold. She ain't just seein' my face—nah, she looks past that, straight to the parts of me I keep hidden, the parts I don't even show myself.

She got the kind of laugh that heals, the kind that makes the bruises fade even when I ain't said a word about 'em. Her joy be contagious, like a balm for the places I don't talk about, like she been here before, like she walked these wounds and came out on the other side, unbroken.

We don't need words most times— but when she speaks, it's gospel, her voice wraps around me like Sunday morning, reminding me that we were born from queens, that our crowns don't slip, that we rise, no matter how many times the world tries to push us down.

She knows the weight of my dreams; how heavy they sit on my chest when I'm too tired to carry 'em. And she doesn't just tell me to keep pushing— she pulls me through it, drags me out of the mud when my legs give out. Her love ain't the fragile kind—nah, it's unshakable, rooted deep, like the oak trees that held our grandmothers' prayers in their branches.

When the world gets cold, my sister be the heat, she burns like truth, like the kind of warmth that can thaw the hardest heart.

Beneath Her Cracked Armor She Blooms

Her arms are always open, like a refuge, a safe house, a place where I can be *me* without apology.

Ain't no question of loyalty— it's written in every "I'm here," in every unspoken gesture, every time she shows up before I even realize I needed someone to stand by my side. She doesn't wait for me to ask for help— she just brings it, holds it out like a gift, reminding me I ain't gotta walk this journey alone.

We hold each other like gospel verses, like prayers whispered into the night, like our mothers' and their mothers' voices stitched into our skin, woven into every step we take, every breath we breathe.

When the storms come, and they always do, we stand together—feet planted, faces to the wind, unmoved, unshaken, because we ain't built to break, we built to rise.

And when the dust settles, when the world goes quiet, my sister don't just know me, she *sees* me. She sees the woman I'm becoming, even when I'm too tired to see it myself. And that? That's the kind of love that outlasts any fire, that outshines any darkness.

My sister, she got me— and with her by my side, ain't no mountain too high, no valley too low, we gon' make it through.

ROSES CAN GROW IN STRANGE PLACES

Don't believe the lie
That roses need perfect soil to bloom.
I've seen them push through cracks in concrete,
Rise from the corners of forgotten streets,
Petals soft as silk against the roughest brick.
They find a way,
Even where they shouldn't.
Even when no one's looking.

Roses grow where you least expect—
In places you thought were barren,
In lives that seem too broken to hold beauty.
They flourish in the shadows,
In the margins,
In spaces where light barely touches.
They thrive on resilience,
Not permission.
And isn't that what makes them beautiful?

It's not the garden that defines the rose,
But the rose that redefines the garden.
It tells the world:
"I am not bound by what surrounds me,
I am not limited by your expectations.
I am beauty in the midst of struggle,
A flower born in defiance of the odds."

Beneath Her Cracked Armor She Blooms

Roses don't need to ask for space—
They take it.
They claim their right to exist,
To grow,
To stretch towards the sky
Even when the world tried to bury them.
They rise,
Not because they were planted,
But because they refused to stay underground.

I've seen roses bloom in alleyways,
In hands that were never soft,
In hearts that were never told they were enough.
I've watched them stretch toward hope,
Toward the impossible,
Turning ugliness into grace,
Turning pain into something sweet.

So, don't tell me where roses are supposed to grow.
Don't tell me what beauty is supposed to look like.
I've learned that life finds a way,
That strength grows in the strangest places,
And that a rose is still a rose,
No matter where it blooms.

SHE TENDS TO HERSELF

    It starts small—
with her checking her body like she checks her phone.
Not just scrolling through symptoms,
but listening.
She hears her own breath and counts it,
      not because she's anxious,
      but because she's learning how to slow down the world
that told her she was always behind.

    She drinks water like it's medicine,
      knowing her ancestors survived off less.
She cooks for herself now,
      real food, not just fast fixes—
      because soul food doesn't come from a drive-thru.
She seasons her greens with intention,
because health is more than kale and yoga.
      It's in the way she prepares her plate—
      feeds herself with things that nourish
instead of things that numb.

She schedules sleep like it's an appointment,
no longer seeing rest as an interruption.
      Gone are the days of being up before the sun,
beating her body into productivity
while her soul stayed weary.
She wakes up when her body says,

"It's time."
And no, she doesn't feel guilty.

Beneath Her Cracked Armor She Blooms

Black women weren't taught to prioritize themselves.
  They taught us to keep going,
like the world would fall apart if we stopped.
  But now?
Now she knows that the world is still spinning
while she's taking her nap,
  and it feels damn good.

Her self-care isn't bubble baths and manicures—
  it's pap smears, therapy,
leaving toxic friendships in the dust.
  It's learning that her 'no' is a full sentence,
that saying yes to herself doesn't require permission
or applause.

She checks her blood pressure before it checks her.
  Doesn't let stress sit in her chest
like an unwelcome guest anymore.
  She knows hypertension runs deep in her family,
so she runs deeper.
  Walks with her head high,
even on days when she's tired.
  She knows that looking after herself
is the most radical thing she can do,
in a world that measures her worth
by how much she can give without breaking.

   Now?
She writes her own prescriptions:
  more joy, less proving.
She follows her own doctor's orders:
  move your body because it deserves to be moved,
not because it needs to shrink.
  Breathe because air is free,

Beneath Her Cracked Armor She Blooms

not because you have to hold it in.
                Love yourself daily, in doses.
Take it slow.

      She unlearned the idea
that self-care is selfish.
Understands now that self-preservation
is not a luxury but a necessity.
      It's not just about living long,
it's about living well.

And when she looks in the mirror,
it's not to find flaws or fix things.
      It's to see the woman she's becoming—
the one who knows that taking care of herself
            isn't a trend,
                    but the blueprint for survival.

This is the real work.
                Not the hustle, not the grind,
but the slow, deliberate act of choosing herself
every day.
She tends to her own garden,
      her own body, her own mind—
           because she knows now,
                  if she doesn't,
                        no one else will.

HOW TO LOVE WHEN YOU'RE BROKEN

Sis,
I see you.
Not the polished, put-together version
they think you are—
but the real you.
The one who's been through fire,
who's held her heart in her hands,
felt it crack,
and still kept walking.
You're tired, I know.
Tired of giving love from a place
that sometimes feels too fragile to stand.
But hear me—
you can love from there.
You must.

You start with the wreckage.
The parts they told you were too far gone,
too bruised, too complicated.
You pick up those pieces,
because they belong to you,
because they tell a truth that no one else can.
Loving when you're broken is slow,
it's deliberate.
It's not about waiting for somebody to validate the cracks.
It's about knowing that even the fractures
make you whole.

Beneath Her Cracked Armor She Blooms

The cracks are where the light gets in, Sis.
That's how your spirit shines through.

You've carried too much,
survived too long,
to wait for someone else to tell you you're enough.
You already are.

You love from the deep, raw place
that remembers the nights you thought you wouldn't make it.
But here you are—
breathing, standing, surviving.
Sis, that's love.
That's strength they can't touch.
You've walked through things
that would've shattered most,
but look at you—
still here, still standing,
still daring to love again,
even when the thought makes your chest tighten.

When you love from this place,
you don't love small.
You love boldly.
You don't cover up your scars,
you let them speak,
you let them be seen.
Those scars?
They tell a story the world needs to hear.
They don't make you damaged—
they make you real.
You don't love in secret,
hiding the bruises under perfect smiles.
You love openly, Sis,

Beneath Her Cracked Armor She Blooms

with the truth of a woman who's learned
that survival isn't enough anymore—
it's time to thrive.

When you offer love to someone else,
you do it with your whole self.
Not the polished parts,
but the ones that are still in progress.
You say, this is me. All of me.
And if they can't hold that truth,
they're not meant for the love you have to give.
You're too big for people
who want something perfect.
You're real.
You're healing.
And that's enough.
Sis, loving when you're broken is a revolution.
It's declaring, *I'm still here.*
I'm still worthy.
And I love myself fiercely, even now.

Your cracks don't dull your shine, Sis.
They've been through the fire,
and they came out glowing.
You love from a place
that holds both the breaking and the mending,
and that makes your love powerful.

So, love yourself first.
Love yourself fully,
even when you're scared.
And when you're ready,
love someone else with that same boldness.
Because broken doesn't mean unworthy—

Beneath Her Cracked Armor She Blooms

it means you've survived,
and now you love with the strength of every piece
you've put back together.

BENEATH HER CRACKED ARMOR, SHE BLOOMS

he's been walking through fire
like it's just another Tuesday.
Ashes clinging to her shoes,
but she's still moving.
Every step heavy with promises that turned to dust,
with love that evaporated,
and fists raised against a world
that ain't never cared enough to stop burning.

They told her to be strong,
to wear armor that never bends—
but nobody taught her
how to grow when everything's falling apart.
So she had to learn that herself—
how to stitch the pieces back together,
even when they don't fit right.

And now?
Here she is, smack in the middle of the battlefield,
no savior, no lifeline, just her.
Bombs still dropping,
ground still shaking,
but her roots?
They go deep, deeper than they know.
Where others crumble,
she stands firm.
Skin tattooed with battles fought in silence,
heart still beating under the weight of it all.

Beneath Her Cracked Armor She Blooms

It ain't that she don't crack—
because she does,
but through those cracks?
She grows.
They thought they left her in ruins,
but she's out here blooming
right in the middle of their mess.
Pushing through the dirt,
reaching for light.

They thought they'd see nothing but ashes—
but nah,
something's growing,
quiet at first,
but then undeniable.

This ain't about being unbreakable—
it's about blooming in spite of it all.
Her armor? Yeah, it's cracked,
but that's where the magic happens.
Through those splits, she rises—
not because she's supposed to,
but because that's what she's made to do.

She's the flower in the middle of chaos,
roots tangled with scars,
petals that've been kissed by flames.
Nobody told her blooming was even possible here,
but she didn't need permission.

She's proof that beauty grows from the broken,
that resilience ain't always loud—
sometimes it's slow,
steady,
the kind that catches you off guard
until one day you realize,
she's still standing
when everything else has fallen away.

Beneath Her Cracked Armor She Blooms

Her armor wasn't meant to stay perfect—
it was meant to protect until it couldn't.
And now?
Through every crack,
something real, something alive is coming through.
She's not just surviving this war—
she's turning it into a garden where she Blooms!

BLACK HEART LAUGHTER

You ever hear a Black woman laugh?
Not that soft, cute chuckle—
I'm talking about that deep, belly laugh,
The kind that shakes the air,
Like she's had enough of the world but still dares to care.
Sis, that laugh ain't just for show,
It's how she keeps moving, even when life says "no."

That laugh is survival,
It's how she takes the mess and makes it livable.
Like when they tell her to "tone it down" at work,
And she just smirks,
'Cause they want her magic without the heat,
Her results without the flavor.
But she knows—oh, she knows—
That laugh is the only thing keeping her off the news later.

You ever laugh so hard you're holding your side,
But deep down, you know it's keeping you from that *other* side?
Like when Auntie asks for her "lil' something" on the phone bill,
And you know she's serious—
But still, you laugh 'cause ain't nobody sending Auntie a dime,
Even though she asks every single time.

It's the laugh in the group chat after a long day,
When you and your girls break it all down,

Beneath Her Cracked Armor She Blooms

About these jobs, these men,
And the drama you're related to.
It's that wine-sipping, side-eyeing laugh,
Where y'all cackle so hard you cry,
Because sometimes laughing at the chaos
Is the only thing keeping you from asking, "Why?"

And don't get me started on the church laugh.
That laugh when Sister Johnson's hat is reaching for the heavens,
And the choir hits notes only dogs should hear.
You catch your cousin's eye from across the pew,
Trying to hold it together, but you already knew—
That laugh is gonna break out,
Even if you're trying to be holy through and through.

A Black woman's laugh?
It's built from years of taking hits,
From being the one who always fixes—
But finds joy in every twist.
It's a laugh that says,
"I'm tired, but I'm still good,"
A sound that moves through pain,
Like only a Black woman could.

It's the kitchen laugh on a Sunday afternoon,
With the smell of greens and stories that always come too soon.
Your grandma talking about way back when,
Telling tales on your mama,
While you sit there thankful Snapchat didn't exist back then.
That laugh is history—
It's the echo of generations who've seen it all,
Yet somehow keep laughing through every rise and fall.

Beneath Her Cracked Armor She Blooms

But when she really lets go,
When she throws her head back,
That laugh shakes the ground,
Like she's claiming her space,
Like she's wearing her crown.
It's a laugh that says,
"No matter what's come my way,
I've laughed, I've lived, I've had my say."

Sis, that laugh?
It's built different.
It's rich, it's bold, it's full of heat.
It turns struggle into stories,
Turns pain into something sweet.
So when you hear it,
You better believe—
She's not just laughing for herself,
She's laughing for everyone who's ever had to leave.

Black heart laughter,
It's freedom in disguise.
A reminder that no matter what they try to take,
She'll rise—
And she'll laugh.
Every. Single. Time.

LOOK GOOD, FEEL GOOD

It's more than a glance in the mirror.
It's a decision.
A declaration that today, you show up as your best self.
The world will try to shape you,
But looking good is how you shape the world back.
It's not just clothes, not just skin deep.
It's the way you wear the confidence beneath it.
When you step out dressed with intention,
You're telling the universe, "I am here, and I will be seen."

The act of looking good isn't about vanity—
It's about command.
There's power in how you choose to present yourself,
How you set the tone before a word is spoken.
When your fit is sharp, when your presence is undeniable,
The world must take notice.
You're not just dressing for the occasion—
You are the occasion.

It's in the way you wear your confidence like armor.
When you feel put together,
There's a subtle shift in your walk,
A silent but clear message: "I own this space."
And it's not about designer labels or price tags,
But the way you turn simplicity into sophistication,
Making every step feel like a statement.
That's power.
Not borrowed, but built.

Beneath Her Cracked Armor She Blooms

Look good, feel good—
Because the world doesn't always reflect back what you deserve.
You become your own affirmation,
The embodiment of strength that radiates outward.
The reflection in the mirror isn't seeking approval—
It's already validated by the way you carry yourself.
The energy shifts when you decide to own your presence,
Not just as a participant, but as a force.

And when you walk into the room,
It's not the outfit they remember,
It's the way you made them feel.
The way the atmosphere bent in your direction,
The way the conversation paused, even for a moment,
Just to acknowledge your existence.
You didn't need to announce it.
Your presence said it all.

Look good, feel good,
Because it's not just about aesthetics.
It's about positioning yourself in a world
That constantly tries to tell you who to be.
You decide.
You control the narrative.
You shape the perception.
And when you look good,
You're already in control of the room before you've even spoken.

So, whether it's the right shoes or the right frame of mind,
Understand that looking good is more than appearance—
It's a form of self-respect,

Beneath Her Cracked Armor She Blooms

A way of telling yourself and the world,
"I am worthy of being seen."

And when you walk out with that knowledge,
There's no obstacle you can't overcome,
No space you can't own.
Look good, feel good—
And watch how the day follows your lead.

LOVE LETTER TO MY STRETCH MARKS

Dear stretch marks,

I didn't always love you.
You showed up unannounced,
Tracing lines across my skin,
Like you had stories to tell before I was ready to listen.
At first, I saw you as a betrayal—
A sign that my body had stretched too far,
Held too much,
Loved too deep,
And broken in places I thought should stay hidden.

But now, I understand.
You were never a flaw.
You were always my map—
A map of growth,
Of becoming,
Of stretching beyond the limits I thought I had.
You are proof that I survived,
That I carried life,
That I loved enough to expand,
And endured enough to heal.

You are not something to be covered or erased.
You are my history,
Etched into my skin with the hands of time.
You remind me that I've lived—
Lived through change, through pain, through transformation.
And for that, I honor you.

Beneath Her Cracked Armor She Blooms

Now, when I trace the lines you've left behind,
I see resilience,
I see beauty in the way I have held the weight of my own story.
You are my reminder that I am more—
More than what the world sees,
More than what I once believed.
I love you now, in all your silver threads and quiet marks,
Because you are me,
And I am enough.

To the way it connects her to her sisters, her mamas, her grandmamas.
It's a gift, a legacy, a revolution,
A Black woman's laughter is a song—
One the world can't help but listen to.

THESE JEANS GOT STORIES

Last week?
These jeans fit like they were sewn for me,
Snug in all the right places,
like they understood my body's spaces.
But today?
Today they're tight, like they forgot who I am,
Acting brand new, like they don't give a damn.

You ever wake up and realize
Life shifted while you slept?
Like the ground beneath you moved,
but no one left a note or a clue.
Now you're standing there,
Looking at your reflection like,
"How did I get this heavy?
When did my hips spread so wide?"
It ain't just the cake.
It's the weight of the days stacked on my back,
The stress creeping in, like thieves in the night,
The things I held tight that should've been left behind.

Yeah, these jeans?
They're more than denim—
They're a metaphor for the stuff we try to squeeze into,
The spaces that no longer hold us,
Dreams that just won't stretch enough.
But that's how it is, right?
One day you're sliding smooth, feeling fine,
The next, you're pulling at the seams,

Beneath Her Cracked Armor She Blooms

And it ain't just what I ate.
It's the extra weight of waiting,
The bloat of carrying expectations not mine,
The pressure to stay the same
When I've clearly outgrown this frame.

But you know what?
Next week, I'll slide back in like nothing happened,
Like the struggle didn't leave its dent.
And that's the truth—
Life shifts again, and again.
But whether tight or free, I rise above.

These jeans?
They've been with me through it all—
The highs, the lows, the stretch, the fall.
They've seen the days I couldn't breathe,
And the days I exhaled like I was born for this.
So today, yeah, they're snug.
But they'll fit again—
Just like I always do.

AFROS AND ALMOND BUTTER

You ever notice how Black women wear their crowns in different ways?
Afros, locs, braids—we don't do this just for style,
This is how we survive,
How we reclaim what they tried to take.
This hair is a battlefield,
And every twist, every loc, every braided strand is a victory.
Each curl whispers a story of resilience,
Of ancestors who never had the chance to be soft.

I wear my afro like armor,
And some of my sisters wear their locs like roots,
Braids like roadmaps to the healing we never thought we'd find.
You think this hair is just hair?
This is history.
It is trauma and healing wrapped up in every coil,
It is Black girls standing tall when the world told us to shrink.

The weight of locs grow heavy with years of struggle
Each one a testament to patience, to endurance,
To watching yourself grow in ways you didn't think you could.
Locs are the language of time,
Of letting go and letting be,
Of learning that not everything has to be neat and polished to be beautiful.

And braids—
Braids are the art our mothers taught us,
Passed down from hands that knew how to create order in

confusion.
We sit between their legs, feeling the tug,
Each pull grounding us back into the earth,
Reminding us that no matter how much we've been broken,
We're still connected to something greater than ourselves.
Every braid is a bond, every plait is a promise
That we will rise, that we will heal.

And the women who said, "I don't need hair to be whole,
I am beauty without boundaries,
Strength with no attachments."
Their skin shines like a moon in midnight skies,
Bold, bare, unafraid to show the world their rawness.
No hair, no armor, just pure, unfiltered power.
They are the women who carry galaxies in their gaze,
Who walk with the confidence of queens,
Because they know, baby, it ain't about what's on your head,
It's about what's inside it.

This scalp has held secrets, held pain,
But it also holds joy, holds healing.
We rub almond butter into our roots not just for moisture,
But to soothe the burns left by those who tried to touch our crowns without permission.
We massage it in, let it sink deep,
A reminder that this hair, this skin, this body is sacred.
We oil ourselves with love because nobody else knows how to love us like we do.

You ever notice how Black women glow?
Like we carry the sun under our skin?
Like no matter how much the world tries to dim us, we still shine?

It's because we've learned to carry our trauma with grace,
To braid our pain into something beautiful.
This is how we heal—
With each loc, with each twist,
We untangle the knots left by generations of hurt,
We reclaim what they tried to take.

My hair ain't just hair,
It's freedom.
It's revolution.
It's me learning that I don't need permission to love myself.
It's me choosing to be soft,
Choosing to heal,
Even when the world tells me to harden.

So, whether I wear an afro, locs, braids, or nothing at all,
I am carrying my history, my struggle, my healing.
And baby, my hair sho gon' look good doing it

THE LITTLE BLACK DRESS

*It sits there, waiting.
Not a spotlight, but a statement.
Not just hanging on a hanger,
But a whisper with an edge,
Ready for the moment it meets the room,
A simple thread of anticipation woven through every fold.*

*You step in, not for the first time,
But every time feels like the first.
The dress doesn't demand—
It suggests,
It asks how much you're willing to show,
And more importantly,
How much you're ready to know about yourself.*

*You know the feeling:
A subtle tension,
That sharp inhale when the zipper climbs—
It fits different tonight, doesn't it?
Like you've grown into something
You didn't realize you were shaping.*

*This dress isn't a mirror,
It's an invitation,
A question about how far you're willing to go.
The color alone absorbs doubt,
Turns second guesses into quiet confidence,
The kind that slips through conversations
Without needing to raise its voice.*

*Every step feels deliberate,
Like you're measuring the weight of your own presence.*

Beneath Her Cracked Armor She Blooms

It's not about how the fabric moves,
It's about how you move within it.
And the way the air shifts when you enter?
That's no accident.
That's gravity taking a moment to recognize who's in charge.

This dress is a nod,
A quiet understanding between you and the moment.
There's no loudness here,
Only subtle precision,
Like a game you've mastered without even knowing the rules.

You walk in, and there's no need to announce it.
The room adjusts itself,
Not because of what you're wearing,
But because of what you're not hiding anymore.
The details?
They don't matter—
It's the pause before someone dares to speak,
The silence that's louder than any introduction.

And that dress?
It's just the beginning.
It doesn't tell your story,
It lets you choose which part to share.
It's not the point—
You are.

You're not dressing to be seen.
You're wearing what needs no explanation,
What stands on its own,
Without pretending to be anything but what it is—
Simple, sharp, and impossible to ignore

SWEETER AND SEASONED

She ain't in competition with them young girls,
'cause she already ran the race.
Lived through lessons that don't fit in IG captions,
seen love that wasn't ready for her face.
        She don't need tight jeans to feel worthy—
                her worth is draped in time,
      wrapped in wisdom that no surgeon's knife can carve.
          They say youth is a crown,
      but she wears her years like jewels,
each one adding to the shine she earned
        by standing tall when the world tried to bend her.
She don't chase trends,
'cause style flows through her veins.
        She made this lane before they even knew how to walk it.
They think her silence is concession,
          but nah, it's just **peace**—
a quiet confidence that only comes
when you've survived storms they can't even imagine.

Her skin? It's soft but seasoned,
like roots too deep for the wind to sway.
She ain't rushing for the spotlight,
'cause she is the light—
walking into rooms like the sun just arrived.
              She ain't pressed about the wrinkles,
                she calls them roadmaps,
          guides to all the places she's been,
        each crease a lesson,
        each line a story
    about how she rose from the mess they tried to bury her in.

The young girls might still be searching—
        for validation, for love, for self.
But she?
    She's already found herself.
    Knows her name, her worth, her magic,
    and no dollar sign can price that.

Beneath Her Cracked Armor She Blooms

She ain't worried about stretch marks,
she calls them stripes,
earned from battles with life
that she didn't just survive—
she conquered.
They talk about beauty in youth,
but don't even see how her scars shine brighter than the skin they praise.
She ain't tryna rewind the clock,
she's in love with the rhythm it plays now.
Each tick a beat,
each year a dance she's mastered.
And when she looks in the mirror,
she don't see what's lost,
she sees what's grown.
She's not here to compete,
'cause she already won.
No trophies needed,
just the reflection of a woman who's lived,
loved,
and learned how to bloom long after the petals were supposed to fall.

Her gray hair? That's wisdom painted in silver.
Her walk? That's experience carried in grace.
She don't need to rush, 'cause she's got time—
time to build, time to rest, time to just be.
And when she speaks,
her voice carries the weight of every year she's lived,
every truth she's earned.

She ain't worried about fading into the background,
'cause her presence don't need noise to be known.
She stands tall,
not against the young girls,
but beside them,
showing them what it looks like to be whole,
to age like fine art—
crafted by the hands of time,
bold enough to be timeless

GOLDEN, NOT JUST PRETTY

You say she's pretty—for a dark-skinned girl—
As if the sun didn't kiss her first,
As if her melanin wasn't mixed with galaxies,
Spun from stardust and earth.

Her skin holds shades you couldn't name if you tried—
Ebony, cocoa, bronze dipped in gold.
A canvas of history, of survival,
A testament to the brilliance of Black.

You stare, like you've never seen the sun rise,
Like her deep hues aren't the reflection of every dawn.
She's not pretty "for" anything—she's beautiful, period.
The world tried to put her in a box too small for her shine.

Her skin speaks in whispers you can't hear—
Soft, yet bold,
Rich in tones that dance with the light,
Bronze that bends but never breaks.

There's magic in every shade—midnight, mahogany,
The type of glow that turns heads,
Not because she fits your idea of beauty,
But because she redefines it, reclaims it, owns it.

Each time the sun sets, she walks through its fire,
Emerging with skin kissed, blessed,
Carrying the warmth of her ancestors in every pore.
Her beauty doesn't come with a comparison,
It's infinite—like the cosmos, like her soul.

Beneath Her Cracked Armor She Blooms

She's not just pretty for a dark-skinned girl—
She's radiant, a force, a universe all her own.
The sun bows to her,
The stars applaud,
And she walks, untouchable, in her shade of glory.

Beneath Her Cracked Armor She Blooms

BUILT LIKE THAT

She ain't no painted canvas.
She's **concrete** with cracks that spill wildflowers—
a block you drive by slow 'cause you can't take it all in at once.
A vibe like when summer heat meet a cold drink,
and somehow, she's both the sweat on your brow
and the ice clinking in the glass.
Her beauty ain't delicate.
It's **heavy**, like grocery bags cutting into your wrists
on a long walk home after the bus left you.
But you carry it anyway,
'cause you know what's inside will feed you for days.
That's her—
not for show, but to nourish.
She steps out the crib like a hood Mona Lisa,
expression unreadable,
but you feel her watching.
A puzzle you can't solve,
but you still trying to figure her out,
like that song you hum but don't know the lyrics to yet.
Her hips got stories that are written about in journals.
Legs like staircases
that took too many people up,
but she's still standing,
still stepping over cracks in the pavement
that swallowed others whole.
She don't trip; she glide.
And when she walks, you feel the rhythm,
like bass through your chest at the cookout,
shaking the ground, but smooth enough
to keep the chicken from falling off the grill.
And her skin?
Her skin ain't just melanin—
it's the color of grandma's Sunday roast,

Beneath Her Cracked Armor She Blooms

dark and seasoned to perfection,
    the kind you can't replicate,
        no matter how much you try.
The recipe was written in her veins,
    marinated in centuries, slow-cooked in patience,
      and when you taste it,
    you know it's got a bite.
      Her love?
  That's the sauce.
    It ain't no store-bought brand;
it's homemade, simmered in a pot that's older than the neighborhood.
But be careful, 'cause too much will burn your tongue.
        You gotta come correct,
'cause she don't water it down for nobody.
        She ain't sweet tea;
she's a hot cup of coffee that wake you up when you ain't ready
to rise.
    And if you ain't careful,
      you'll be hooked, fiending for just one more sip.
Her laugh ain't no dainty thing either—
    it's loud, like dominoes slapped on the table,
      or when somebody hits a number on the lottery,
and the whole block knows.
It fills the air, bouncing off bricks,
echoing in the spaces where silence once sat.
        She don't need no mirrors or makeup—
  her reflection is in the way she make you feel.
      A gut check,
like the first day of school with no new shoes,
    but somehow, she still the flyest in the room.
        And when she smiles,
it's like finding twenty dollars in the pocket of jeans you forgot
    you had,
      pure joy,
unexpected, but you hold onto it like you knew it was yours all
along.
    You can't box her in—

Beneath Her Cracked Armor She Blooms

her beauty don't fit in no Instagram frame.
She ain't just curves or lips or hips.
She's a whole blueprint,
a building with windows that don't show everything inside,
but if you lucky enough to get in,
you better act like you know what to do with the key.

Her sex appeal ain't in the glance,
    it's in the way she keep you coming back for more,
like the bodega on the corner that stay open when the world
closes down.
    A convenience you didn't know you needed,
    until nothing else satisfies that hunger.
    She's the hunger and the food,
    the chase and the calm after.
    Ain't no need for her to dress it up—
she could walk into a room in a headscarf,
house shoes flapping on the linoleum,
and still command the floor like she in heels.
    Her presence is a flex,
    and she don't even need to say it.
    You feel it.
    Like when the power goes out,
and all of a sudden, you realize how much light you were living
in.
    She ain't pressed to be in nobody's line-up,
ain't checking for nobody's approval.
She been approved by the universe,
    stamped by the hands that built the pyramids.
    She knows her worth,
    like she keep a receipt in her back pocket,
    ready to return any man that ain't full price.
    Her beauty ain't what you see,
it's what you feel—
    like that good night's sleep
you didn't know you needed.
    She's rest in a restless world,
but don't get it twisted,

' cause when it's time to move,
she ain't waiting on nobody.

Her sex appeal ain't loud,
it's the kind that lingers,
like the smell of cocoa butter on fresh skin,
like that last note of a song you ain't ready to let end.
She's the encore before you even know you clapping.

BROWN SUGAR HONEY POT

There's sweetness in her,
A richness that lingers,
Brown sugar, slow to melt,
But once it does, it sticks.
It's not loud, not rushed,
Just a quiet kind of heat
That simmers beneath the surface,
Soft and smooth,
Like a secret you're dying to taste.
Her love is honey-thick,
The kind that drips slow,
Golden, warm—
It clings to you long after you've touched it.
You think you know sweet,
But until you've tasted her,
You've only known sugar by name.
She's that depth,
That richness,
That honey pot you only find
When you've learned how to be still,
How to savor what takes its time to give.
Her body speaks in whispers,
A language of curves and skin,
And if you listen close enough,
You'll hear it—the hum,
The way her softness sings
Like a melody wrapped in satin,
Like sugar cane pressed and stirred,

Beneath Her Cracked Armor She Blooms

Her sweetness never comes easy—
It's earned.
It's in the way her hips sway,
In the way she lets you in,
Not too fast, not too soon.
She gives you a taste,
Just enough to leave you wanting more.
That honey pot?
It's sacred ground,
Brown sugar melting on your tongue,
But never all at once.
You've got to take your time,
Let her sweetness unfold,
Because rushing won't get you closer,
And nothing this sweet is for the impatient.
She's the kind of woman
Who turns touch into poetry,
Who makes you crave the honey you didn't know you needed.
Her love flows like molasses,
Slow and deep,
And once you've tasted it,
You'll never settle for anything less.
Brown sugar honey pot—
That's her essence.
She's not just sugar,
She's a whole damn recipe,
A sweetness that's complex,
A richness you feel in your chest.
And if you're lucky enough to taste,
To sip from the pot,
You'll know there's nothing sweeter,
Nothing more divine
Than the honey she holds within.

RED LIPSTICK

She slicks it on like war paint,
a bold, unspoken declaration,
her lips glowing against her skin—
dark like mahogany, like earth rich with history.
Red lipstick, the kind they used to whisper about,
say it was for women of the night,
for those too wild, too bold, too free
to fit into the mold they wanted.
"Red lipstick ain't for good girls,"
they'd mutter,
eyes narrowing,
and the words landed like weight on our mothers,
our aunts,
our grandmothers—
Black women holding their tongues
for fear that this world already thought too little of them.

But look at us now,
painting our mouths crimson,
not for their gaze but for our own reflection,
for the way it makes our skin glow like fire under a dark sky.
We wear it for the ones who couldn't,
for the ones who bit their tongues
because society told them that boldness belonged
to someone else,
to the ones who were told to stay in their place
but knew deep down that they were more.
We wear red as a reminder
that we've always been more.

They said red was for whores,
but baby, we've reclaimed it—

Beneath Her Cracked Armor She Blooms

turned it into armor,
into power,
into the signature of every Black woman
who's ever been told she was too much
but knew she wasn't enough in their eyes.
The kind of woman who walks into a room,
lips painted with defiance,
eyes sharp with purpose,
hips swaying like they own the ground beneath them,
because they do.

We wear it for them, too—
the ones who clutched their pearls
and warned us to be careful,
who never understood that red is not just a color,
but a revolution.
That the gloss and shimmer
hides a history of women who refused to dim,
who painted their lips
and let the world wonder how it got that bright.

And isn't it funny,
how something as small as a tube of color
can hold so much meaning,
so much history wrapped in a shade
meant to be loud and unapologetic?
Because that's who we are.
Black women have always known
how to make something out of nothing,
how to turn what they feared into something fierce.

So here's to the red,
the rouge they said was too much,
the color they tried to keep from us
as if they could steal our shine.
Here's to the Black women who wear it now,
with skin deep like night,
with pride in their stride,
with lips painted like a sunrise—

Beneath Her Cracked Armor She Blooms

radiant, bold, uncontainable.
We wear it because we can,
because we choose,
because we are,
and no one can tell us otherwise.

NOW, I UNDERSTAND

Jody's mama, hands deep in the soil,
Planting seeds like she was planting hope.
I didn't get it back then—
Why she spent so much time in the garden,
Talking to plants like they held her secrets,
But now I understand.
It wasn't just flowers she was growing,
It was peace.
It was the one thing she could nurture,
In a world where everything else was trying to take something from her.
In that garden, she was free,
Turning dirt into beauty,
Trying to make sense of a life
That didn't always bloom the way she planned.

And I think about Stony,
When she sat in that car in *Set It Off*,
Tears mixing with the money she'd earned at the cost of her soul.
Back then, I thought it was just about the struggle,
Just about getting out,
But now I see it was about **sacrifice**.
How Black women give and give,
And sometimes, even after giving everything,
They still end up with their hearts in pieces.
Stony wasn't just trying to escape—
She was trying to reclaim the parts of herself
That the world kept telling her she didn't deserve to have.

Then there's *Waiting to Exhale*,
When Bernadine set his stuff on fire,
Watched it burn like her broken dreams.
I didn't understand the fire then,
But now?
Now I know it was freedom,
It was release.
The flames weren't just consuming the clothes—
They were consuming the hurt, the betrayal, the lies.
She needed to watch it all go up in smoke,
Needed to clear space for the woman she was becoming.
It wasn't just anger—
It was survival.

And *The Color Purple*,
When Celie looked Mister in the eyes and said,
"Until you do right by me…"
That wasn't just a curse;
That was the stripped voice of every Black woman
Celie wasn't just fighting him—
She was reclaiming her voice,
Her power.
I get it now—
That scene was about **self-worth**.
About knowing that you are more than what someone else decides for you.

I think about those moments now,
How they felt so big, so heavy,
But I didn't have the words to understand them.
Now I see the beauty in the resilience,
The grace in the fight,
The way these women found themselves

Beneath Her Cracked Armor She Blooms

In the cracks, in the pain,
putting out her own fires

These scenes were more than just great actors—
They were about creation.
They were about getting back to her something beautiful
About Black women turning the broken pieces of their lives
Into something whole,
Something full
Jody's mama wasn't just planting flowers—
She was planting herself.
And every one of those women,
In every scene,
Was learning to bloom

THAT AIN'T THAT

They tell you femininity is quiet.
Obedient. Like I'm supposed to sit pretty,
all while they fumble the bag,
the relationship, and my respect.

Real femininity is power.
It's knowing when to relax,
and knowing when to stand tall—
because being a woman ain't about playing small
to fit into no man's idea of what I should be.

Want a woman to submit?
Give her something to submit to.
We don't bow for weakness in a man.
Don't fold for ego dressed in insecurity.
A *high-value man*?
Well, he fully understands
it ain't just about his wallet or how many books he read.
It's how he holds his woman, catches her when she falls,
it in how he shows up when it's time.
How he handles life's weight without asking her to carry it all.

Submission is earned.
Not by control or your bank account.
It's by showing you can handle what black woman will bring,
'cause she don't come in pieces—
She come whole.
Comes with history, strength,

Beneath Her Cracked Armor She Blooms

a love so deep it could heal you—
if you know how to receive it.

But here's the kicker:
She can't rest in you if you don't know how to lead.
And I ain't talking about bossing her around.
I'm talking about making her feel like she can trust you
to have her back,
to make decisions with y'all in mind,
to protect, provide, and be present.

These social media prophets?
They got it twisted.
Acting like submission means weakness,
Like it's something to be ashamed of,
Like a woman must lose herself just to keep a man.
But submission? It's trust.
It's knowing she can lean into him
Because he's steady.

I see women bending over backwards,
Doing acrobatics just to make it work,
Holding it all together when he's giving the bare minimum.
They want us to call that love?
We're supposed to stay quiet?
They call us "angry" when we speak up,
When we demand more than scraps.

If being angry means standing up for what I need,
Then hell yes, I'm angry.
I'll wear that like a badge of honor,
Because I know my worth.
And my femininity?
It's not fragile.

Beneath Her Cracked Armor She Blooms

It's wood for my fire,
The kind that burns through anything fake.

I don't want to be strong all the time.
I want to be held.
I want to feel safe.
But that takes a man who knows what safety means,
Who isn't afraid to protect what he loves,
Who doesn't see my strength as a threat,
But as a gift, not a requirement

"ALL THAT ENERGY"

Let's talk,
not in whispers but in the language only we know,
the kind that moves in rhythm, like hips swayin' to beats we
ain't gotta hear.
This ain't no game of "what he said,"
this is about what we feel, what we deserve.
Don't nobody understand us like we do—
the way we've carried nations on our backs,
sustained empires with our hands,
and still, somehow, they question our softness,
like we ain't tasted the salt in our own tears
and turned it into sugar when no one was looking.

We don't fall for half-hearted attempts—
we need more than just touch.
More than that fleeting fire they call desire.
See, when you come for a Black woman, you gotta come
correct—
come with that mind first, that spirit second,
'cause we've been healing too long
to settle for surface-level love.

We know what real energy feels like,
it's that quiet storm that shakes the room
without makin' a sound.
It's the knowing glance we give each other when he's all talk—
you feel me?

Beneath Her Cracked Armor She Blooms

Don't come at me with noise,
I need that real connection, deep like roots,
the kind that nurtures you from the inside out,
feeds you soul food without you even knowing you were
starving.

I need a man that reads me like a book with no pictures,
one who knows my edges are sacred
and my silence is not an invitation.
Touch my spirit, baby—if you want me to open.
Love me with the kind of care that honors the queens before
me,
that whispers to the ancestors like, "I got her."
'Cause when you hold a Black woman,
you're holding generations—
do you have the strength for that?

Don't talk to me about passion
if you can't speak the language of patience.
I need more than fast hands and quick breaths—
give me intellect, give me intention, give me purpose.
We deserve love that moves mountains,
not just shifts sheets.
Love that sings with its mouth closed,
that knows when to sit in silence with you,
when to build altars instead of breaking promises.

So, bring all that energy—
but don't rush.
I'm a Black woman, I move in my own time,
and trust, baby, when you finally earn this,
you'll know the difference
between a storm and the calm that comes after it.

DATE 'EM ALL SIS

Listen, sis,
Lonely don't mean desperate,
And tired don't mean settle.
Just because your aunties are whispering,
And your phone stays dry on a Friday night,
Doesn't mean you need to be running down the aisle
With the first man who texts back.
Marriage ain't a cure for being alone—
It's just another layer to the journey,
And baby, you're still writing your own story.

Date 'em all, sis.
That's right, try them on for size.
'Cause the dating pool? It's got a little pee in it,
And let me tell you,
You gotta wade through some shallow waters
Before you find anything worth swimming in.

I'm talking about the 20-year-olds with big dreams
And no plans.
The 40-year-olds with daddy issues and a savings account,
But can't hold a conversation deeper than a tweet.
You'll meet the talkers, the smooth ones,
The ones who can charm you right outta your good sense,
But baby, don't be fooled—
Charm don't pay bills, and it sure as hell don't feed the soul.

Beneath Her Cracked Armor She Blooms

You ain't too picky.
Nah, sis, you're seasoned.
Dating at 40 don't look like it did at 20,
When red flags looked more like carnival rides,
Exciting, dizzying, and worth the thrill.
But now?
You spot them from a mile away,
Like, "Nah, I see that game. I played it and won already."

This ain't about a ring on your finger,
It's about the love in your heart.
You're not just looking for someone to stand next to—
You're looking for someone to grow with,
And that takes time.
So date 'em all, sis.
See what fits.
You're not here to settle just 'cause you're tired of waiting,
You're here to build something real.

And if they ask why you're still single,
Look 'em dead in the eye and say,
"I'm not waiting for love, baby, I'm building it."
You see, lonely don't scare you—
You've been loving yourself too long to mistake it for weakness.
You've learned the art of your own company,
How to pour wine and run a bath just for you.
So don't let them rush you.
You've got standards,
And they're not too high.
You're just not playing small anymore.

Go on, date 'em all.
Swipe left, swipe right,
Slide into the DMs if you must—

Beneath Her Cracked Armor She Blooms

Just remember, you're not auditioning for a man.
They're auditioning for you.
Let them prove they can handle your light,
Your laughter, your layers.
Because it's not about finding someone to complete you,
It's about finding someone who complements
The masterpiece you've already become.

So, sis, if you're 30 or 40 or 50 and still looking?
Don't you dare feel rushed.
You're not running out of time—
You're refining your taste.
And when the right one comes?
You'll know.
Not 'cause he ticks every box,
But because he'll walk beside you in love,
Not drag you into it.

Until then?
Date 'em all, sis.
Try 'em on like shoes,
And if they don't fit?
You keep walking, head high,
Because lonely don't mean desperate,
And tired don't mean settle.

Beneath Her Cracked Armor She Blooms

"WHY WE DON'T TEXT BACK"

It's not that she didn't see your message,
she did.
It's just that time has taught her—
her energy ain't free,
and her words?
More valuable than a 2 a.m. "wyd"
from someone who barely knows her middle name.

She used to respond out of politeness,
used to hold space for those
who didn't deserve a seat at her table.
But she's learned since then.
Now, her silence is a shield,
not to be mistaken for rudeness,
but for self-respect.

You see, she's mastered the art
of keeping her peace intact,
of not wasting time on empty conversations,
half-hearted attempts,
and the low-energy offers
that never held weight in the first place.

Maybe you think she's being petty,
but really—
she's just tired of explaining herself
to people who ain't even listening.
She's grown past the need
to entertain folks who wouldn't know how to handle her truth.
Her phone?
It's got enough receipts of things left unsaid,
because not everything needs a reply.

Beneath Her Cracked Armor She Blooms

What's she doing instead?
Baby, she's living.
Out here building an empire,
handling her business,
caring for her soul.
She's at brunch with her girls,
laughing loud,
sipping mimosas,
talking about the new goals she's setting—
the kind of dreams that don't have time
for breadcrumb texts.

You thought a "hey beautiful"
would keep her hooked?
Nah, she's looking for something deeper,
something more than just the surface-level sweet talk
that fades as fast as it came.
She needs consistency,
conversation that doesn't feel like she's pulling teeth
just to get to the heart of it.

She's not ghosting you,
she's just prioritizing herself,
making sure her time goes
to the things that matter most—
her growth, her joy, her peace.

Because if there's one thing
a Black woman knows,
it's that her time?
Is priceless.

And if you can't bring more than a half-thought reply,
or match her energy with intention and respect—
don't expect her to hit you back.
She's got bigger things to focus on
than playing games
with men who never learned how to show up.

Beneath Her Cracked Armor She Blooms

So, if you're wondering why she's gone quiet—
it's because she's busy being loud
about her life,
about her dreams,
about herself.

"SWIPE LEFT ON RED FLAGS"

1. He says, *"I'm not ready for anything serious,"*
   but he keeps texting after midnight,
   sliding into your DMs like it's a habit,
   but can't seem to slide into any real commitment.
   Red flag disguised as "let's keep it casual."
   Girl, swipe left—
   you know he's not ready for what you deserve.
2. His phone stays on silent,
   but somehow, he's always *"busy."*
   Never picks up,
   but has time for you when it's convenient.
   Red flag with a side of ghosting,
   don't let him haunt your peace.
   Your time is precious,
   and a man who can't make space for it
   doesn't deserve to waste it.
3. He says, *"My ex was crazy,"*
   but every story sounds like a blame game.
   Red flag dipped in gaslighting,
   'cause somehow, every woman in his life got it wrong—
   except him.
   Sis, run—
   you're not here to fix his past,
   you're not a therapist for his unresolved mess.
4. *"You're overthinking it."*
   Nah, sis—
   your intuition is screaming,
   and he's just trying to quiet it down.
   Swipe left on the man who tries to tell you
   that your gut feeling doesn't matter,
   'cause you know when something ain't right.

Beneath Her Cracked Armor She Blooms

    You were born with that sixth sense,
    don't let him dull it.
5. *"I've just been really busy."*
    Too busy to call, to text,
    but somehow not too busy to watch your stories,
    like he's got all the time in the world to monitor your moves.
    Red flag?
    More like a whole parade, waving proudly.
    Girl, you deserve someone who makes time,
    not excuses.
6. He's still living with his *"ex,"*
    but they're just roommates now,
    sharing rent and "space" but not "feelings"—
    at least, that's the story he tells you.
    Red flag wearing rose-colored glasses,
    and you know better than to fall for that trick.
    Don't let him confuse your kindness for foolishness.
    Swipe left before you end up playing house
    in someone else's game.
7. *"You're different than the other girls."*
    Compliment wrapped in a red flag,
    setting you up like you're a prize on a pedestal.
    But you know better—
    he's not comparing you out of love,
    he's putting you in a box,
    waiting for you to fit his narrative.
    Swipe left—
    you're no one's "better option."
    You're the main story, not a plot twist.
8. He calls you *"too independent,"*
    but what he really means is,
    you don't need him the way he needs to be needed.
    Red flag for his fragile ego,
    'cause a man who can't handle your strength
    will try to break it.
    Girl, your independence is not a threat—
    it's a blessing.
    Swipe left on any man who tries to make you feel otherwise.

9. He says, *"Why you gotta post that?"*
   Suddenly, he's monitoring your moves,
   policing your selfies,
   acting like your freedom of expression is a problem.
   Red flag holding the keys to control,
   watching your every step like he owns the map.
   Swipe left,
   before he tries to shrink your shine
   or turn your glow into something that serves him.
10. *"I just don't do titles."*
    But he's treating you like a placeholder,
    keeping you on hold
    while he figures out his next move.
    Red flag wearing indecision like it's cute,
    stringing you along like you're just another option.
    Swipe left—
    you're not waiting around for clarity
    when you deserve certainty.
11. He talks about *"building"* but doesn't lay a single brick,
    just promises that never turn to action,
    dreams that stay stuck in neutral.
    Red flag wrapped in potential,
    but you know better than to fall for a blueprint
    without any follow-through.
    Swipe left—
    you're not here for empty foundations.
12. *"I'm not the jealous type,"*
    he says, but the way he checks your phone,
    the way he side-eyes your friendships—
    it tells another story.
    Red flag dressed up in false confidence,
    but his insecurity leaks out
    like a faucet you can't turn off.
    Swipe left on the man who says he's secure,
    but can't handle your light.
13. *"We're just talking."*
    He loves to keep things "open,"
    loves the gray area

where nothing has to be real or defined.
Red flag in limbo,
keeping you guessing about where you stand,
but you know you're worth more than mixed signals.
Swipe left—
you deserve someone who doesn't make you question
what you mean to them.

14. *"I don't really believe in marriage."*
He says it like he's enlightened,
like commitment is beneath him.
Red flag trying to sound woke,
but what he really means is,
he doesn't want to settle down—
at least, not with you.
Swipe left—
you deserve someone who isn't afraid
of building a future.

Each red flag is a warning,
a signal waving brightly,
telling you to trust your gut,
to honor your worth.
Swipe left on every man
who tries to dull your shine,
who doesn't meet you where you stand.
Because, sis, red flags don't change color—
they just wave louder the longer you ignore them

I AIN'T MARRIED, BUT IF I WAS

I ain't married, but if I was,
I'd probably be the type to start a fuss
Just to see if he could handle me—
Not the soft, sweet me, but the wild me,
The me that forgets to fold laundry but never forgets her dreams.
I'd need someone who knows how to step to the edge,
Who's not afraid to hold me close
When I'm feeling a little too far from myself.

    If I was married, I'd be the one to burn the toast,
        Laugh it off,
    Then ask if we're getting takeout tonight.
    I'd leave sticky notes on the fridge,
    Little reminders that love ain't in the grand gestures
        But in the everyday stuff—
    The way we sit together after a long day,
    Not saying much but knowing everything.

        I ain't married, but if I was,
    He'd have to know how to read me like a favorite book,
        The kind you keep coming back to,
            Finding new layers,
        Even when the pages are worn.
He'd have to understand that my silence ain't distance,
        It's just me thinking too hard,

                              And he wouldn't rush me.
                                  He'd let me breathe.

                        If I was married,
            We'd dance in the kitchen to songs we forgot we loved.
                    We'd argue over who's washing dishes,
        Then end up laughing about something that don't make sense.
                        And when things got tough?
            He'd know how to hold me down without holding me back.
                        He'd let me be, let me fly,
                 And when I came back, we'd sit down,
                              Break bread,
                    And rebuild whatever fell apart.

I ain't married,
But if I was,
He'd know I don't need saving,
Just someone to remind me that I'm already whole.
Someone who sees the magic in the mess,
Who loves me through the chaos,
The calm,
The in-between.
If I was married,
It wouldn't be perfect,
But it'd be real.
And maybe, that's the best kind of love.

"Love Me When I'm Quiet"

Love me when the world fades out,
when my voice isn't rising above the noise,
but sinking beneath it.
Love me when I'm quiet—
when the glow dims,
when the spark you saw in me isn't shining
the way it used to.

It's easy to love in the light,
in the noise,
when we're laughing,
when the world's clapping for us.
But can you love me
when I'm still?
When the hustle slows down,
when my energy isn't enough to carry us both,
when I'm just here,
being,
existing in silence?

Love me in those moments
when I don't have the words,
when I'm not "on,"
when my body's tired from all the battles
I never spoke of.
Love me when I'm not fighting,
but just breathing,
when my spirit needs rest,
not revolution.

It's easy to show up
when life feels like a celebration,
when my smile is wide
and the world is watching.
But will you stand beside me
when the room is quiet?

Beneath Her Cracked Armor She Blooms

When there's no applause,
no accolades,
just us,
in the stillness
of a day that feels like too much?

I don't need you to save me,
just to hold me,
to remind me that I'm worthy of love
even when I'm not pouring it out.
Love me when I'm quiet—
when my strength looks like softness,
when my fire takes a breath
and the world feels heavy.

Because love,
real love,
isn't about the noise.
It's about the peace,
the comfort of knowing
I'm enough,
even when I'm silent.

"MEN ARE NOT PROJECTS"

She learned,
after too many nights spent holding together pieces
that weren't hers to fix,
that men are not projects.
She's not a toolbox,
not some blueprint for redemption,
not the answer to every wound they refuse to heal.
It's not her job
to sew together hearts that never wanted mending,
to sand down rough edges
just so they feel smooth enough to hold.
She's tired of being the fix-it woman,
the one they run to when the world breaks them
but won't stick around when it's time
to build something real.
They come in broken,
expecting her to be the cure,
thinking her love is glue,
her time a remedy
for the wounds they never tended to.

But no more.
She's not a rehab center
for men who won't even admit they need saving.
She's not here to be the lifeline
for someone who's already drowning
but won't reach out for help.
She's done being the woman
who always has to be strong
while they crumble,
done being the one who pours
while her own cup runs dry.
Men are not projects,
and she's not the architect of someone else's growth.
If he can't stand on his own,

if he can't meet her where she stands—
whole, steady, ready—
then he's not worth the time it takes
to watch him fall apart.
She's not looking to fix,
to patch up what someone else broke.
She's looking for a partner,
not a puzzle.
And if he comes with too many missing pieces,
that's on him, not her.
She's learned that love
doesn't mean being a crutch,
doesn't mean breaking herself
to put someone else back together.
She's whole on her own,
and she's not here to be the one
who makes someone else feel complete.
Men are not projects,
and she's done building
what was never hers to build.

"LOVE LOOKS DIFFERENT NOW"

Love doesn't look the way it did at 20.
Back then, it was all fireworks,
bright lights and loud promises,
a rush of feelings that couldn't wait
to burn out.

Love looked like urgency,
like I had to chase it,
catch it before it slipped through my fingers.
It felt like a game I needed to win,
like the louder it was,
the more real it must be.
But now?
Love looks different.
It's quieter,
more deliberate.
It's not about proving anything,
not about fitting into a story
someone else wrote.
Love doesn't demand as much now.
It knows its place,
knows that it doesn't have to shout
to be felt.
It's in the little things—
the way you check in without being asked,
the way you listen
even when the words are hard to find.
It's in the space we give each other,
the patience to grow,
the understanding that love is a process,
not a destination.

I used to think love meant fixing,
saving,
rescuing someone from themselves.
But now?

Beneath Her Cracked Armor She Blooms

I know love is about standing beside them,
letting them be,
loving them where they are,
not where you wish they would be.

Love used to look like grand gestures,
like flowers and declarations
meant for everyone to see.
But now it's in the quiet moments,
in the way you show up,
in the way you let me be soft,
let me rest.
Love doesn't look the way it did
when I was trying to impress,
trying to hold onto something
that wasn't meant for me.
Now, love looks like peace,
like coming home to myself,
knowing that I deserve more
than the bare minimum.
It's not just about passion anymore—
it's about presence.
It's about choosing someone
who chooses you back,
not just when it's easy,
but when life gets hard,
when the world isn't looking.
Love looks different now,
because I've grown.
I've learned that love isn't a prize
to be won—
it's a partnership,
a quiet, steady hand
that holds you through the chaos,
and reminds you
that you're enough,
just as you are.

"I KNOW WHY I STILL SING"

I know why I sing now,
not because the cage held me down,
but 'cause I got used to the weight,
learned how to dance with chains clinking like broken promises,
how to make rhythm out of rust.
I didn't just hum to stay sane—
I built songs out of survival,
out of the scraps they left me with.
See, I ain't no victim,
I'm the blueprint for resistance.

I know why I still fly,
even when the world put bricks on my back,
made me heavy with expectations I never asked for.
They tried to tell me my voice was too loud,
like I wasn't born to break ceilings.
Told me to smile more,
to sing sweet, keep the rage soft.
But I ain't no lullaby.
I'm a war cry in the middle of a quiet room,
I'm the storm that comes when you think the rain's done.

The cage?
It's not my story—
it's just where they tried to hide me.
But c'mon now,
they should've known better—
a bird born with rhythm don't forget how to move.
So I found freedom in the middle of their bars,
learned to bend my song into something
that could slip through cracks,
flow like water,
rise like steam off the heat they tried to bury me under.

Beneath Her Cracked Armor She Blooms

They ain't ready for this kind of tune,
'cause it ain't sweet.
It's got basslines heavy with history,
high notes that cut like truth,
melodies wrapped in resistance.
I ain't singing for peace,
I'm singing for power,
for the girls they tried to keep quiet,
for the boys they silenced before their voices even broke.

I know why I keep singing—
'cause it's the only way to break the chains they think I still wear.
I ain't just flying for me—
I'm flying for my mama,
who carried weight that wasn't hers,
for my grandma,
who taught me how to take a whisper and make it thunder.
For the ones who ain't got no wings,
but still find a way to soar.
I'm singing for every soul that had their notes stolen,
for every caged voice that never got to scream.

And don't get it twisted—
I don't sing soft,
don't sing nice.
I sing raw,
'cause that's how it needs to be.
I'm spitting verses that burn,
breaking down walls with a melody laced in truth.
I don't want your applause,
I want your reckoning.
I ain't here for your peace—
I'm here to wake the dead,
to shake the earth
until the cracks let us breathe.

The cage?
That's history,

Beneath Her Cracked Armor She Blooms

and I'm already rewriting it.
I know why I sing, Maya,
'cause they tried to bury us
without knowing we were seeds,
and I'm here, blooming,
loud and unapologetic,
a symphony they can't silence.

Beneath Her Cracked Armor She Blooms

WHERE MY GIRLS AT

It started with the beat—
a pulse we carried, heavy like history,
back when "ladies first" was more than just a hook,
it was respect, the crown on our heads,
the gold in our skin.
We built the stage, set the scene,
but somehow, our stories got lost between the basslines.
They dropped our names, left us faceless,
and we still asking, "Where my girls at?"

Hip hop became the soundtrack of our fight,
but the same brothers we stood beside
turned the mic into a weapon.
We went from "keep ya head up" to "b*tches ain't sh*t,"
like our worth was something to be flipped,
like we ain't hold the whole culture on our hips.

Megan said it's a "Hot Girl Summer,"
but who's feeling the burn?
We lit the fire, but now we're the ones getting scorched,
dancing to the same tracks that call us out our name,
moving to beats that break us down,
turning empowerment into a game of survival.

I see us—
queens turned into props,
swag drippin', but where's the respect?
When did we start mistaking a bag for dignity,

letting the beat box us into something smaller,
something less?

We raised them, fed them,
stood in the front lines,
and now we're the bodies bent over in the back.
The ones who laid the bricks for this foundation
now watching them build walls around us,
and we still standing outside, knocking.

I can't lie—
there's power in the way we move,
the way we reclaim space in a culture that erases us,
but I can't help but wonder:
When did the love songs turn into battles?
When did the rhythm start reflecting the cage?

It's psychological—
how they fed us their narratives,
made us believe the only way to win
was to play by their rules.
We hopped on the bandwagon,
but who's driving?

We wear the bars like armor,
but who wrote the verse?
We spit their words,
and now we're stuck in a loop,
calling it empowerment,
but is it really freedom when the chain still glints under the gold?

We the ones who built this—

Beneath Her Cracked Armor She Blooms

don't let the lies tell you different.
Hip hop wasn't born to break us.
But they turned the music into a mirror
that only reflects what they want us to see.

I'm saying,
they convinced us to dance for them,
but the song was always ours.
We hold the melody in our veins,
and it's time to remind them—
we ain't just the hook, we the whole damn verse.

WILLIE LYNCH AND US

They told us it was a myth,
but we know what's real when it lives in our bones.
The Willie Lynch letter—
written like a script for how to break us down,
how to pit us against each other,
how to take Black women,
queens in their own right,
and turn them into pieces of something unrecognizable.
They say it was just words,
but those words turned into chains we didn't see.

They told us divide and conquer.
Keep the young against the old,
the light against the dark,
the women against the men.
And we've been carrying that weight
since before we could name it.
How does that live in us now?
Look at the sisters who don't trust other sisters,
the ones who think they gotta fight
for space that should've always been ours.

How does it feel to walk in a world
that says you're too strong to be soft,
too loud to be loved,
too much to be understood?
They broke us down so we wouldn't stand together,

so we'd look at each other with suspicion
instead of seeing the power that pulses in our blood.
They made us think we had to be hard,
when all we ever needed was to be whole.

You feel it, don't you?
The way they set the stage—
"Make her depend on no one.
Make her carry the load alone,
so she'll never think to ask for help."
Now, here we are,
generations later, still trying to heal from wounds
we didn't even know were cut.

But what if we asked the questions they never wanted us to ask?
What if we said, "Why do you want us to hate ourselves?"
Why do you fear Black women so much
that you had to create a blueprint
for how to break us down, piece by piece?
Why do you try to erase the softness in us,
the brilliance, the magic, the love?

Because they knew—
they knew that if we ever realized who we are,
the whole system would fall.
The letter wasn't just about control,
it was about fear.
Fear of what happens when Black women
stand in their power,
when we see each other not as rivals,
but as reflections of something unbreakable.

Beneath Her Cracked Armor She Blooms

So here's what I'm telling you,
my sister, my reflection—
we don't have to live under the shadows
of something written to destroy us.
We are not the product of their fear,
we are the answer to it.
We were never meant to be divided.
Our strength isn't in being hard—
it's in being whole.

So I'm asking:
What happens when we love ourselves again?
What happens when we see our skin,
our bodies, our voices
not as things to be silenced or made small,
but as the loud, vibrant truth of who we are?
What happens when we rewrite the script?

They said we'd be broken forever,
but they lied.
We've been rising,
even in the cracks, even in the pain.
We rise because we were never meant to stay down.
We rise because their words don't define us.
We rise because our power can't be stolen,
even when they tried.

So today, I speak to the Willie Lynches of the world—
your time is done.
We see your chains,
and we've learned how to break them.
We're not divided,
we're united,
and we're claiming what was always ours.

Beneath Her Cracked Armor She Blooms

Black girl, Black woman—
you are more than what they said you'd be.
You are the answer to every lie they tried to make true.
Stand tall.
Speak loud.
Love hard.
Because this world wasn't built for us,
but we're rebuilding it
with our hands, our voices, our truth.

And no letter,
no lie,
no system can stop that now

ARMOR IN EXCELLENCE

There was a time when these hands weren't allowed to hold books,
When our minds were seen as fields to be tilled but never nurtured.
We weren't supposed to read,
Weren't supposed to know our own power,
But we found ways.
We carved knowledge into the cracks of the walls they built around us,
Passed down wisdom in whispers,
And hid freedom in pages we weren't supposed to turn.

Black women have always been a revolution in motion,
An armor made of letters and language,
Of stories we weren't supposed to know,
Of truths they tried to keep hidden.
But we dug up those roots.
We traveled through dark nights guided by the stars,
Not just following the North Star to freedom,
But chasing the light of knowledge that would break every chain.

They said we weren't meant to read,
But we read anyway.
We taught ourselves in secret,

Sat in dark corners with candles flickering,
Letting every word, every sentence become a weapon
To fight the lies they told us about who we were,
About what we could be.

We were Harriet before we knew her name,
Navigating the tunnels of their ignorance,
Running from the plantations of mental slavery,
Mapping out our own freedom
One chapter at a time.
Books became our Underground Railroad,
And we passed knowledge like coded messages—
One sister to another,
One generation to the next.
We turned education into liberation,
Built schools from nothing,
Because we knew that to teach one of us
Was to free all of us.

Our education wasn't a privilege;
It was an act of war.
Every Black woman who cracked open a book
Was rebelling against a system built to keep us small.
And now, we stand on the shoulders of those who refused to be silent,
Who refused to be erased.
We sit in classrooms that our ancestors could only dream of,
But we know this is not just a seat—it's a throne.
Every degree, every diploma is our crown,
And our knowledge?
That's the armor we wear into every battle.

We are the daughters of women who learned to read in secret,
And we don't take this lightly.

We know that every page we turn is a victory,
Every test we pass is a triumph,
Because we weren't always allowed to be here.
But we're here now.
And we are learning for those who couldn't,
For those who had to hide their brilliance beneath headscarves and aprons,
For those who risked everything just to know something more.

We are Harriet's dream,
Sojourner's hope,
The fulfillment of the promise our ancestors whispered to each other
When they were running through the night.
We carry books like torches,
Lighting the way for those who come after us,
Knowing that our education is not just for us—
It's for every Black girl who will follow,
Every sister who will stand where we stand
And push the line even further.

Armor in excellence—
That's what we wear.
A Black woman with knowledge is unstoppable,
Unbreakable,
And undeniable.
We have learned too much,
Fought too hard,
To ever be silenced again.
So, we read.
We study.
We rise

Beneath Her Cracked Armor She Blooms

Sleeping Beauty

She was asleep,
not in some fairytale tower,
but in her own bed,
breathing the kind of peace we chase after long days.
And they came for her—
without a knock,
without a warning,
just a burst of gunfire,
turning her dreams into dust.

Breonna Taylor didn't die with a chance to fight,
she was stolen from her sleep—
a Black woman's rest always under threat,
'cause it seems even in our most private moments,
they find a way to make us a target.
No warrant worth her life,
no justice for the bullet that knew no reason,
only force.

How many more?
How many Black women taken in the dead of night?
48 just in 2020.
That's the number they'll print,
but numbers don't bleed.
Numbers don't hold the weight of mothers collapsing at gravesites,
of fathers burying daughters who should've been safe at home.
The numbers lie—
they don't capture the echo of each shot fired
in the hearts of the living.

"Say her name," they chant,
but how many names do we carry now?
Tatiana Jefferson,
killed in her own home for nothing but suspicion.

Beneath Her Cracked Armor She Blooms

Rekia Boyd,
gone in the night, no camera to show her innocence.
Korryn Gaines,
shot in front of her son like her life wasn't sacred.
The list is heavy,
but this world?
It acts like the weight don't matter,
like our lives are disposable,
like Black women don't make good headlines
unless we're lying flat on the pavement.
You ever notice they don't talk about us
unless we're dead?
They don't show our joy,
don't capture our beauty,
just the bloodstains left behind.
That's the legacy they paint for us,
like the only way we're important
is if we're martyred.
They don't tell the stories of our dreams,
of the lives we were building,
of the families we carried on our backs
while this system kept taking.
48 Black women,
in a single year,
snuffed out by a system that don't even see us.
But what about those we never hear about?
The ones who didn't make the news,
who didn't get the protest signs,
who slipped through the cracks
of a society that never cared to look twice.
They told us to trust the law,
but the law's hands are stained with our blood.
Police don't knock,
they break,
and we're left to pick up the pieces—
or more likely, someone's left to pick up our bodies.

Beneath Her Cracked Armor She Blooms

What do you tell the families?
That justice is slow?
That her life just wasn't enough to make them care?
How do we breathe in a country that keeps choking us out,
hands around our necks whether we're awake or asleep?
We ain't safe anywhere.
Not in our homes,
not in the streets,
not in the courtrooms where our killers walk free.
Breonna was supposed to wake up.
She was supposed to live.
She wasn't supposed to be a hashtag,
but that's the world we live in—
where Black women go to sleep
and don't get to see morning.
Where our beauty is only recognized
once we're no longer here to claim it.
No prince kissed her awake.
The system kissed her with bullets,
took her breath like it was theirs to take.
And for what?
A lie? A mistake?
How do you mistake a life?
How do you misplace the worth of a woman who did nothing wrong
but exist in the wrong skin?
Korryn, Rekia, Sandra, Aiyana,
they never made it to their tomorrows.
Black women are tired of marching for tomorrow,
tired of lighting candles for daughters we never got to meet.
And what do we tell the next generation?
That the world might come for them while they sleep?
That the cost of Blackness
is always knowing you're one bullet away from being a memory?
Breonna Taylor,
Tatiana Jefferson,
the names haunt us,
but their ghosts don't rest.
Their souls march with us,

Beneath Her Cracked Armor She Blooms

not for revenge,
but for a reckoning.
This is the reality—
no flowers, no sweet refrains,
just truth laid bare:
We live in a place where sleep is dangerous,
where the night can swallow you whole,
and justice is a dream we keep chasing
but never catch.
But we will never stop calling them back,
never stop shouting their names until the world shakes,
until the system breaks,
and Black women
no longer have to die
to be heard

Beneath Her Cracked Armor She Blooms

FOR KAMALA AND THE SISTERS IN POWER

She stands at the podium,
not just for herself,
but for the ancestors,
the ones who never thought they'd see the day
a Black woman would stand in the halls of power,
in rooms where they once counted us less than human.
Kamala, a name whispered through generations,
carrying the weight of every Black woman
who dared to dream in a world that told her, "No."

This isn't just history—
this is reclamation.
A seat at the table that was never built for us,
in a house we weren't supposed to enter.
But here she is,
standing firm,
with the echoes of chains long broken,
and the sound of ballots cast by hands that once couldn't vote.
This is the revolution wrapped in pearls and power.

The *Declaration of Independence* was never written for us.
"We the People" didn't mean *our* people.
It was inked in freedom they kept for themselves,
while we were the property they sold.
They said all men were created equal—
but forgot to mention the chains,
the auctions,
the cotton fields,
the screams of mothers torn from their children.
America, built on our backs,
still tries to turn a blind eye to its own reflection.

But here stands Kamala,
here stand the Black women in power,
not by permission,

Beneath Her Cracked Armor She Blooms

but by persistence.
They came for us in the dead of night,
stole our bodies,
tried to steal our souls,
but didn't know we carried fire inside.
We were never supposed to make it this far—
but they underestimated the strength of a people
who survive everything.

From Harriet's footsteps on the Underground,
to Shirley Chisholm breaking every ceiling,
to Michelle, with grace under the weight of the world,
and now Kamala,
carving a new path with every word,
every move.
We are the revolution they can't silence,
the uprising they never saw coming.

They didn't want us to learn the law,
to speak in courts,
to write the policies that shape this land.
But we studied.
We learned.
We rose.
Now we're in the rooms they tried to keep us out of,
drafting the future they swore we'd never touch.

Kamala's voice isn't just her own—
it's the collective scream of Black women everywhere,
saying, "You will not erase us.
We belong here.
This was ours, even when you tried to tell us it wasn't."

Slavery was the blueprint,
but freedom?
Freedom is the remix.
We were written out of the history books,

Beneath Her Cracked Armor She Blooms

so now, we write ourselves back in—
with ink, with votes, with power.

She stands,
with every syllable steeped in the blood of our foremothers,
and the sweat of every woman who scrubbed floors so her daughters
could dream.
This is not just a Black woman in politics—
this is a revolution in heels,
walking into spaces they said were closed,
reminding them that we never needed their keys.
We build doors where walls once stood.

Kamala,
and every sister standing beside her,
they are not just politicians—
they are promises kept.
They are what happens when the ones you counted out
become the ones you count on.
They carry the torch for the ones who couldn't run,
for the ones whose voices were silenced.

The *Declaration* never spoke our names,
but now?
Now it has no choice but to listen.
Because the revolution is here,
and she's wearing pearls,
and she's got a pen in her hand,
and she's rewriting everything.

WE WANT WHAT'S OWED

They never told you what really happened on those ships,
did they?
How they snatched us from our lands,
stripped us of names,
packed us like cattle into darkness,
and dared to call it a journey.
But it wasn't a voyage.
It was hell.
A hell where Black women were nothing but flesh,
bodies bound and broken before we ever touched land.

They don't talk about the screams below deck—
about the men who came down at night,
tore our clothes, ripped our dignity,
took everything we had left.
They came to take,
and take,
and take.
Some of us—God, some of us—
chose the ocean.
The sea was cold, but it was freedom,
and how twisted is it that death felt like a better option
than whatever waited on the other side of that shore?

We jumped,
because the water couldn't hurt us like they did.
We jumped,
because we refused to let them own our last breath.

Beneath Her Cracked Armor She Blooms

They don't teach that part in schools,
how Black women were the first to fight.
How we were warriors before they even knew our strength.

And then they took us to plantations—
and if you thought the ship was bad,
you ain't seen nothing yet.
They used us up,
turned our wombs into factories for their empire.
We birthed their children while our own were sold,
while our hearts were ripped from our chests,
our babies torn from our arms.

They raped us.
Let's not sugarcoat it.
They took what they wanted,
left bruises, left scars,
and called it their right.
How do you heal from that?
How do you forgive a world that never asked for forgiveness?

Sarah Baartman.
They paraded her like an animal in a circus,
examined her, judged her,
made her body a spectacle
because they couldn't understand it,
because they couldn't control it.
And even in death,
they wouldn't let her rest.
They cut her open,
preserved her like some kind of trophy,
as if her life meant nothing more than their twisted curiosity.

Beneath Her Cracked Armor She Blooms

What did slavery do to Black women?
It turned us into survivors.
But not because we wanted to be.
Because we had no choice.
We were beaten, broken, and still expected to stand.
They burned our history,
but they couldn't burn our spirit.

How do we move forward?
Tell me.
How do you move forward when the past ain't dead?
When the pain is stitched into your blood,
when every generation feels the weight of chains
even though we ain't wearing them no more?

We move forward by demanding.
Not asking.
We move forward by remembering,
by reclaiming everything they tried to steal.
This isn't about turning the other cheek—
we've been slapped enough.
This is about taking what's ours,
what we built, what we bled for.

Black women were never just victims.
We were revolutionaries,
we were the heartbeat of the movement
before it had a name.
We are the daughters of warriors,
the mothers of nations,
and we demand what's owed.

So yeah, we want reparations,
not as a handout, but as a damn payment

Beneath Her Cracked Armor She Blooms

For the ship,
for the chains,
for the babies they stole,
for the bodies they raped,
for the blood they spilled.
for the lives we were forced to live,
for the dignity they stripped away
like it was theirs to take

But we also want our story told.
We want the world to know what they did
and what we have lived through,
Because we are still here,
standing,
fighting,
refusing to be erased

CURRENCY AND CHANGE

Before we could speak our own names,
we were a dollar sign, a line in somebody's ledger.
Economics wasn't a class we could skip;
it was written into our skin, traded like sugar cane
and cotton we picked but never owned.

But we flipped it.
We always flip it.
Turn chains into gold,
side hustles into survival,
and yeah, corner store candy into capital.

See, they don't know how we hustle.
How we took those skills they underestimated—
braiding hair in kitchens, frying fish on Fridays,
flipping cases of water in traffic
just to keep the lights on.
We turned nothing into enough.
We made a way when all we had was our hands
and the knowledge they never wanted us to have.

And now?
Now, we build empires.
Not with bricks, but with braids, with shea butter and a plan,
with lashes and logos, LLCs and love.
We've been sold, bought, and sold again,
but now? We buy back the block.

No more leases, no more renting somebody else's dream.
We want deeds in our hands,

not just rent receipts.
You think entrepreneurship is a trend?
Sis, it's in our DNA.
We've been making magic out of kitchen beauty
long before it was Instagrammable.

But this ain't just about side hustles—
it's about real power.
Ownership. Legacy.
They sold us, broke us, and we built back.
We're not asking for reparations;
we're making them with every house we buy,
every business we own,
every dollar we flip from struggle into something permanent.

You see us?
We aren't just getting by.
We create wealth, we invest in ourselves,
because the economy we live in wasn't made for us—
but we make it work.
We flip systems the same way we flip houses—
from redlined to redefined,
and our children?
They won't inherit struggle.
They'll inherit keys.

Harvard can't teach us this—
what we know can't be found in textbooks.
It's found in mothers who worked two jobs
and still made it to parent-teacher conferences,
in grandmothers who owned homes
without ever stepping foot in a bank.
It's found in the way we turned beauty into billion-dollar

Beneath Her Cracked Armor She Blooms

brands,
in the way we flipped markets they thought we'd never touch.

This is about more than getting by—
it's about getting ahead,
owning the land we stand on,
the businesses we run,
the future we build

A BLACK WOMAN'S VOICE & CHOICE

What is freedom,
If not the right to claim my own?
If not the power to decide my path,
To shape the seeds I've sown?
What is a voice,
If it's drowned beneath the laws they make,
If my choice is stripped before it's given,
If my body's not mine to take?

Roe v. Wade wasn't just a law,
It was a shield against control,
A reminder that my womb is sacred,
That my body's not a toll.
I'm more than just a vessel
For a world that isn't ready,
I'm more than just a means to life,
While the weight they place is heavy.

They call it justice,
But where's the justice for me?
When Black boys are cuffed before they're men,
And Black girls can't run free?
You say it's about the sanctity of life,
But whose life do you mean?
When the streets devour the very breath
Of the children I've never seen.

Beneath Her Cracked Armor She Blooms

You want to legislate my being,
Tell me how and when to give,
But how can you call it freedom
When it's my body that you refuse to let live?
I choose when to bring life forth,
I choose when the soil's been tilled,
For bringing a child into this world
Is more than a dream fulfilled.

It's not just about survival,
It's about building something new.
A future where my children thrive,
Not one that's stacked against you.
To take my choice is to take my voice,
And silence what's been long denied—
That Black women have the right to live,
To choose, to rise with pride.

This body's mine, not yours to claim,
Not a tool for your agenda.
You speak of morals, of life, of laws,
But where's your true defender?
Where's the justice for the women
Who are told they must comply?
Who live in fear that their own choice
Will be stripped before their eyes?

You see, it's not just about my womb,
It's about the legacy we leave.
It's about the world we build for those
We choose to birth and grieve.
And I will not be reduced to this,
A pawn in a game you play.

Beneath Her Cracked Armor She Blooms

I'll stand with those who've come before
And speak for them today.

The choice to give life is sacred,
But the choice **not** to is just as divine.
I choose to walk my path in peace,
To draw the boldest line.
For a Black woman's voice is power,
And our choice is a song we sing.
You cannot take what's rightfully ours,
We are queens, and we wear the ring.

So, hear me when I say it loud,
My choice, my voice, my will.
You can try to strip it all away,
But my spirit? You can't kill.
Roe v. Wade was not the end,
It's the battle we still face,
And as long as Black women walk this earth,
We'll fight for our rightful space.

MISSING WITHOUT A SOUND

Every 6 hours, a Black girl goes missing.
Do the math—
that's four girls a day, 28 a week,
112 a month, and by the end of this year,
over 1,400 Black daughters, sisters, mothers, will vanish into thin air.

And.... you won't hear a word.
60,000 Black women and girls are gone.
Missing.
Not missing like misplaced keys,
not lost like a stray dog wandering the neighborhood.
Gone. Taken.
From Chicago to D.C., Atlanta to Houston,
snatched from their lives like they never existed.
135 Black girls missing in Atlanta—
just the last six months.

And what have you heard?
Nothing.
Because the headlines don't stretch for us.
79 gone in Baltimore,
173 in Chicago.
D.C., the nation's capital?
91 of our girls erased like yesterday's news,
like they don't matter enough to find.
109 missing in Houston,

but you'd swear the only thing missing is the system's conscience.

What's more disturbing than the numbers?
The silence.
They label her "runaway,"
as if running is the only option she has left.
But this country loves to run away from accountability.
Black girls are 40% of all missing women,
but we make up only **13%** of the U.S. population.

Explain that math.
Explain why we go missing in higher numbers
but get found at a fraction of the rate.
Because when a Black girl vanishes,
she doesn't make the 5 o'clock news.
She doesn't get the nationwide alerts,
the social media outcry,
the 24-hour cycles that other faces get.
She gets forgotten.
Filed away under "problematic" or "at-risk."
They say she'll "show up"
like a misplaced wallet.
We know the truth.

The system was never designed to search for us.
Black bodies are disposable.
We are the forgotten daughters of America's selective empathy.
This isn't incompetence—
this is a deliberate decision to ignore us.
To erase our stories because they don't sell papers,
don't boost ratings.

We are the **60,000** missing souls
whose names you don't know.
We are the 60,000 faces that never made it past local news,
because the media loves its blonde-haired, blue-eyed tragedies,
and we don't fit the mold.
We know what happens to Black girls who go missing—
they disappear into the cracks of a broken system,
into a pipeline of human trafficking,
where **40%** of all trafficking victims are Black.
That's nearly half.
But where's the national coverage?
Where are the task forces,
the search parties,
the nationwide outcry?
Where are the dogs?
Where are the helicopters?
Where are the bodies in the streets looking for our bodies?

This ain't just negligence—
this is genocide.
The system isn't broken—
it's working just how it was designed.
To overlook us.
To write us off as "missing" without ever searching.
But let me tell you something—

Black girls are abducted, trafficked, sold—
their skin becomes a commodity.
We are missing,
but it's not just a physical disappearance.
It's systemic erasure.

Our lives are disregarded by a system that sees us as collateral damage.
The world is quiet because her screams don't echo loud enough in
these halls of justice.

We are not invisible.
We are here.
We have always been here.
And every day that passes,
another girl slips into the void.
But not on our watch.
We will shout her name,
we will shake the walls of this system,
we will not rest until every Black girl missing
is brought back home.
We refuse to let the silence win.
60,000 Black girls missing.
But we will not be ignored

A BLACK WOMAN THAT LIVES ON THE SUN

They say, if you look up at dawn's first light,
You can catch her silhouette—
A Black woman dancing on the sun,
Twisting fire into braids,
Weaving flames into gold threads,
Her laughter echoing in every sunrise.

Legend has it, she's been there since the beginning,
Long before the world knew her name,
Long before the sky learned to hold her glow.
She was born in the heart of a solar flare,
Birthed from the heat of a million stars.
They say she never needed wings—
The sun itself lifts her higher.

They call her the Bringer of Light,
The Mother of Flames,
The one who kisses the earth each morning,
Warming the skin of the people she loves most.
She doesn't just rise—
She commands the day,
Spinning the sun like a crown,
Casting shadows wherever she pleases,
Because she controls what grows,
And what withers.

Folks say, when the world gets too cold,
When winter overstays its welcome,
She steps down from her throne,

Beneath Her Cracked Armor She Blooms

Pulls the sun closer to earth,
And whispers, "Enough."
Her breath melts the snow,
Her eyes burn away the frost,
And spring returns at her call.
They say without her,
There'd be no harvest,
No flowers,
No fruit,
Just endless night.

But she's no gentle goddess—
Her power isn't just to nurture.
She's the fire that blazes through fields,
Clearing the old to make way for the new.
When anger stirs in her belly,
Storms swirl in the sky,
And the sun turns blood red,
A warning to those who forget her name.
Her fury scorches the earth,
Reminding all that she can destroy
Just as easily as she gives life.

Children whisper stories about her at dusk,
How she guards the balance between light and dark,
How she'll burn anything trying to throw it off.
"Don't play with the sun," they say,
"Or you'll feel her heat in ways you weren't ready for."
Mothers tell their daughters,
"Look to her when you need strength,
When you need light in the darkest of days.
She watches over us,
A protector we don't always see,
But always feel."

Beneath Her Cracked Armor She Blooms

The elders say she's older than time,
Older than the earth itself,
And they call her by names long forgotten,
Passed down from mouths that knew her before books were written.
They say she is the keeper of dreams,
The light in the souls of Black women,
The eternal flame that burns in each of them.
She lives in their laughter,
Their warmth,
Their resilience.

And when the sun sets low,
When the sky is awash in fire and gold,
That's when you can see her best—
A Black woman standing on the sun,
Hands on hips,
Head held high,
Her fire casting light across the world.

She doesn't ask for worship,
Doesn't need praise.
She's the quiet force,
The constant presence,
The heat that gives life,
The flame that makes us whole.
And they say, no matter how far the darkness stretches,
She'll always be there,
Dancing on the sun,
Turning day into night,
And night into day.

A BLACK WOMAN'S PRAYERS

My prayers ain't soft whispers,
They're battle cries wrapped in grace.
Every 'Dear God' comes from a place of struggle,
From wounds I've patched up myself,
From nights when silence was louder than hope,
But I pray anyway—
Because a Black woman's prayers don't stop when the world does.

I pray with my fists clenched,
Knuckles bruised from holding it all together,
Pray for my son,
For my daughters,
For the ones I ain't even birthed,
But carry in my heart because that's what we do—
We hold the world on our backs and pray we don't break.

I pray for strength,
Not the kind they think I already have—
Not the 'you're so strong' that tastes like backhanded compliments,
But the strength to keep loving,
To keep pushing forward when every system is built to make Me stop.

I pray for peace,
Not the 'just be quiet and endure' kind,

But the kind that lets me rest without my mind racing,
Without counting the things, I need to fix,
Without wondering if my prayers will reach beyond the ceiling.

I pray for my sisters,
For the ones whose names won't make headlines,
Who won't get marches or hashtags.
For the ones still fighting battles that ain't theirs to fight.
I pray they see their worth,
That they know they're more than the struggle,
More than the burdens placed on their shoulders.

I pray for the men—
For the ones we lost to the streets, to cells, to silence.
I pray for the ones still here,
Trying to rise but slipping on the mess the world leaves behind.
I pray for their protection,
Not just from bullets and brutality,
But from the demons they carry in their own minds.

I pray for the babies,
For the sons who will grow into men too soon,
For the daughters who will carry their mother's burdens too early.
I pray the world is kinder to them,
That they won't have to pray like I do—
With their backs against the wall,
With fists raised in silent defiance.

I pray for love,
For the kind that doesn't ask me to shrink,

That doesn't mistake my strength for invincibility.
I pray for love that doesn't run when things get heavy,
That holds me up when I can't carry it all.
I pray for the love that reminds me I'm human,
That I deserve softness too.

I pray for healing,
For the wounds passed down from generation to generation,
For the scars we wear like armor.
I pray we find peace in places we were taught to fear,
That we reclaim the softness they tried to steal.

I pray for justice,
But not the kind they write about in law books—
I pray for the kind that lives in our bones,
The justice we create for ourselves when the world won't.
The justice that says we are enough,
That our stories matter,
That our voices ain't just background noise.

I pray for days where I don't have to pray so hard,
Where joy comes easy,
Where the world ain't so heavy on our shoulders.
But until then,
I'll keep praying,
Because a Black woman's prayers are more than just words—
They're survival,
They're revolution,
They're the fire we carry,
Even when the world tries to put us out.

ABOUT THE AUTHOR

NaKiyah LaJoi is a mother of three—two young adults and an 11-year-old—and a proud Lola to a sweet Black grandson. Born on the West Coast and raised in Washington, DC, NaKiyah's life has been marked by struggle, trauma, and the healing power of writing. Her journey began at the age of nine when her father gifted her a pink diary with a brown elephant and a lock—a safe space where she could pour out her thoughts, fears, and dreams. That diary became her refuge, her lifeline.

Over time, writing became more than just an outlet—it became essential to her survival. She filled journals with songs, poems, prayers, and pep talks, each entry reflecting her path toward healing, growth, and self-discovery. For a long time, her writing was private, a sanctuary where she could be her truest self without fear of judgment. As she evolved, so did her voice. Today, NaKiyah shares her words with the world, understanding that her story—like countless Black women—carries power, healing, and truth.

"I wrote this book to tell the story of pain, healing, growth, motherhood, and the journey from girlhood to womanhood," NaKiyah shares. "It celebrates our Blackness, rich history, traumas, and resilience. It's for women in every season of life—empowering them to embrace and celebrate each step of the journey."

Beneath Her Cracked Armor She Blooms

NaKiyah's book is a testament to the complexities of being a Black woman—balancing joy and pain, trauma and resilience. It highlights the strength, beauty, and grace Black women carry and serves as a reminder that despite life's struggles, Black women continue to rise and create beauty from adversity. "Our journeys aren't always glitter and rainbows, but we still make rainbows and find our pot of gold."

These poetic stories are for Black women everywhere because we all carry pieces of the same truth. We are worthy of love. We are worthy of healing. We are worthy of taking up space in a world that often tries to shrink us. Poetry is my way of reminding us of that.

From the little girl with her pink diary to the woman she is now, writing has been NaKiyah's way of navigating life. And with *Beneath Her Cracked Armor She Blooms*, she hopes to inspire Black women everywhere to own their stories, love themselves fiercely, and remember that beneath all the armor, they have the power to bloom.

Currently a full-time student studying elementary special education and working as a Community Health Worker, NaKiyah is dedicated to uplifting her community and future generations. Through her writing, she offers a voice of empowerment, healing, and sisterhood, honoring the stories of Black women across all walks of life and generations.